"Charleston has a landscape that encourages intimacy and partisanship. I have heard it said that an inoculation to the sights and smells of the Carolina low country is an almost irreversible antidote to the charms of other landscapes, other alien geographies. You can be moved profoundly by other vistas, by other oceans, by soaring mountain ranges, but you can never be seduced. You can even forsake the low country, renounce it for other climates, but you can never completely escape the sensuous, semitropical pull of Charleston and her marshes."

—Pat Conroy

Sweet Carolina
MYSTERIES

Roots and Wings

Sweet Carolina
MYSTERIES

ROOTS
~~~ and ~~~
WINGS

Kathleen Y'Barbo

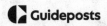

Sweet Carolina Mysteries is a trademark of Guideposts.

Published by Guideposts
100 Reserve Road, Suite E200
Danbury, CT 06810
Guideposts.org

Cover and interior design by Müllerhaus
Cover illustration by Bob Kayganich at Illustration Online LLC.
Typeset by Aptara, Inc.

This book was previously published under the title *Where Mercy Begins* as part of the *Miracles & Mysteries of Mercy Hospital* series.

ISBN 978-1-961126-65-7 (hardcover)
ISBN 978-1-957935-55-3 (epub)

Printed and bound in the United States of America
10 9 8 7 6 5 4 3 2

ROOTS and WINGS

To Renee—Rosarian, Researcher, and Master Gardener
And to Sharen for reasons she knows. I'm glad at least
the right thing has happened in fiction.

But the seed in the good soil,
these are the ones who have heard
the word with a good and virtuous heart,
and hold it firmly, and produce fruit
with perseverance.

—Luke 8:15 (NASB)

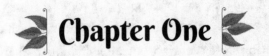

Chapter One

IT WAS THE BEGINNING OF a beautiful June Tuesday in Charleston. The cool of the night had not yet given way to the heat of summer, and the ever-present sea breeze rustled the leaves of palm trees permanently bent inland. The unpredictable spring weather was behind them, and the heat of July had not yet arrived.

Joy Atkins spent the two-block walk from her home to work as she always did—praying about the coming day and being grateful for the beauty around her. Straight ahead was the Charleston Harbor. She could just see the shoreline peeking around the old wing of Mercy Hospital, her destination. Halfway there, she looked left and caught a glimpse of Rainbow Row—a line of historic row houses painted in pastel colors that reminded her of the Caribbean.

"Good morning, Mercy." Joy smiled up at the Angel of Mercy statue that had graced the south side of Charleston's Mercy Hospital for as long as anyone could remember—longer than anyone who walked this path had been alive. For this beautiful and modern hospital had its roots in the original building, which was built in the 1820s. The statue was lovingly situated in a beautifully landscaped area with flower beds and several benches where staff sometimes came to take their much-needed breaks.

Mercy was old by most standards but not here in Charleston, where age was a measure of pride—at least in statues and buildings. If only it worked that way for people.

Joy patted the statue's foot and winked at the beautiful stone woman, a habit she'd acquired soon after coming to Charleston and taking the job at Mercy Hospital's gift shop. For the past several months she'd been taking a detour to the south side of the hospital every morning to greet the angel before backtracking her way to the front entrance. While she no longer required daily treks past the statue in order to gather her thoughts and find solace in her new role as a widow and her new life managing the shop, she kept up the habit of visiting the old girl because she found her to be good company and an excellent listener.

Not that the ageless Angel of Mercy looked old. Rather, she was beautifully young with smiling features and a kind face that radiated happiness. A strange way to describe a statue made of stone, and yet it was true.

One look at the angel and Joy could smile, no matter if the news of the day was good, bad, or somewhere in between. Thus, it only seemed right to offer some response. And though the angel had never returned the gesture, Joy half expected to get a wink back someday.

Someone else must have agreed with Joy's assessment of the statue, for occasionally a beautiful Noisette rose, a pale cream bloom with a crimson center, was waiting when she arrived at work. Perhaps it was a tribute to the angel or, possibly, to someone else. Either way, the appearance of the rose always prompted Joy to pray for the person who left it.

She retraced her steps to the front of the building and the main entrance. As the automatic doors opened to admit her into the hospital's lobby, she shifted the bundle of freshly cut flowers from her garden so as to keep the delicate iris blooms safe from accidental jostling. Though her official job was manager of Mercy Flowers and Gifts, she often became a supplier as well when she supplemented the floral inventory with blooms from her own little patch of abundance. Wilson had called her love of gardening endearing, although he certainly must have had his moments when whatever she was growing that season took over their yard and nearly all available indoor space as well.

What a wonderful man, her husband. When questioned, Wilson would refer to all the greenery, flowers, fruits, and vegetables as Joy's Abundance. Thus, any spot where she put in a garden was her patch of abundance. Wilson had even taken to his woodshop—that small space he'd carved out of their garage where no plants were allowed—to make a beautiful wooden sign. Even now, the JOY'S ABUNDANCE sign held a place of honor in the rear garden of her new house after the movers had transported it more than a thousand miles away from the home she'd shared with Wilson.

"Good morning, Joy," her friend Evelyn Perry called as she hurried past, likely headed to her office in the Records Department.

"Good morning to you," she responded.

Evelyn paused to look at Joy. "Oh, those irises are beautiful. Mine aren't blooming yet."

Joy smiled. Evelyn was a busy working woman with a full life and a job that often required her to work long hours. Though she and her history professor husband had no children of their own, it hadn't taken Joy long to see that Evelyn had become surrogate grandmother to uncounted numbers of the hospital's youngest patients. She loved flowers, but the growing of them was another subject. Joy had an entire section of her garden devoted to plants she had rescued from Evelyn in just the past few months.

"Did you fertilize like I suggested?" she asked her friend, already suspecting she knew the answer.

Evelyn returned her grin. "I handed that job over to James, so I don't know. Say, are you free for coffee around ten? I've got something I'd like to talk to you about, and it's not flowers. Actually, I'm thinking of putting together a wedding shower for Nancy Jones, a sweet nurse up in maternity. She's getting married soon, and I don't think she or her young man have any family here to give her any sort of send-off into marriage."

Joy nodded. "Coffee sounds great. See you then."

Evelyn offered a wave before ducking into the hall on the opposite side of the building from the elevators. Joy hurried on, her pace slowed by the people milling about the lobby, her favorite place of the entire hospital other than the gardens.

Joy looked skyward, as was her habit, and smiled. Overhead, a painted blue sky with wisps of clouds remained from the original building and made the space always sunny no matter what the weather was outside. An ancient gas lamp, now electrified, hung from the center of the ceiling, its cut crystal pieces dancing in the breeze from the air conditioner and showering the gloriously veined white marble floor with spirals of tiny rainbows.

The lobby's modern touches blended perfectly with the beautiful antique doors and stained-glass windows that marched along walls covered in ancient cypress panels and dotted with artwork done by the patients over the years. In pride of place on the mezzanine of the second-floor walkway was an Alfred Hutty original painting depicting Mercy Hospital as it looked in the early 1900s.

Just like the city itself, Mercy Hospital had perfectly blended old and new, modern and antique. And though she missed Texas and the life she'd shared with Wilson, she was quickly falling in love with her newly adopted home. If only she could find her place here—the spot where she belonged. She chuckled when she thought of something Evelyn had told her. When Alfred Hutty first came to Charleston after serving in World War I, he had wired home to his wife, "Come quickly, have found heaven."

Another glance at the painting above and she smiled. She'd known the move here was meant to be. Now she'd just have to muster up a bit of the patience she too often lacked to find out just why He had planted her here.

Juggling the flowers and her purse in order to retrieve her keys, Joy lost her grip on both. The keys went sliding on the marble floor while the flowers and her purse landed at the feet of Dr. Chad Barnhardt, an emergency room physician.

"Here, let me help. I'll get these. You go find those keys."

Tall with sandy brown hair that faded to silver at the temples, Dr. Barnhardt was known for his strict adherence to the rules and his penchant for long hours and hard work. He also had a nice smile despite a reputation for being a bit of a grump on occasion.

The doctor gallantly scooped up the flowers and then snatched up her purse while Joy chased after her keys, which had become wedged behind an oversized urn filled with greenery. A moment later, she let herself into the shop and turned on the lights.

Dropping her keys into her pocket, Joy gratefully accepted the flowers and purse from the doctor and took them to the back of the store. Stowing her purse under the antique counter that used to be the hospital's front desk during the first half of the previous century, she gently laid the irises out in front of her.

"Thank you so much." Joy gave him an appraising look and found his handsome face etched with what could only be exhaustion. "Won't you sit down and have a cup of coffee? It's on a timer so that it starts brewing just about the time I get here. There's nothing more lovely than fresh coffee on a beautiful morning."

He gave her a grateful smile as he leaned against the doorframe. "I'd like that, but I'm on my way home to catch some sleep."

"Another twenty-four-hour shift?" At his nod, she continued. "Oh my stars, I don't see how you doctors manage it. I know there are places for y'all to hide and catch a nap, but I just couldn't go that long without a proper eight hours."

Dr. Barnhardt's smile faltered. "I vaguely remember what eight hours of sleep is like. The need for it is successfully trained out of us somewhere between studying for our MCATs and the first year of medical school."

"Bless your heart," she said. "You need to take a vacation."

He straightened and shook his head. "Not while we're under-staffed and there's a hiring freeze going on. No one's getting any time off. I know you believe in miracles, so maybe you should pray that the board increases our budget for the next fiscal year so we can hire some help. Even a few well-qualified interns would be welcome."

There it was. Another reminder of the hospital's budget issues and the accompanying hiring freeze. Joy mustered a smile.

"Well now," she said. "I most certainly can do that, but then you know I'm always happy to pray for you."

The doctor gave her a sideways look. The subject of prayer had quickly become a sore one between them. Joy knew the man standing before her would one day give up on his lack of faith and accept what she already knew, namely that the Lord loved him and was worthy of love from him in return.

But she had been gentle in her prodding and respectful in their conversations. Thus, while Dr. Barnhardt seemed resistant to faith, he was apparently not resistant to the occasional mention of it from Joy.

A bell rang behind her letting Joy know the coffee was ready. She held up her hand. "Wait right there," she said, her Texas drawl creeping through. "I'll be back in two shakes of a lamb's tail." She hurried to the back room and poured the doctor a cup. "Here ya go, honey. Black coffee, no cream or sugar," she told him when she reappeared.

His grin broadened. "Just the way I like it. How do you remember these things?"

Joy shrugged. "I just do. Now go home and get some rest. But take a few sips on your way so you don't fall asleep before then, please."

"Yes, ma'am," he said as he accepted the coffee and headed toward the door, weaving his way through a rush of shoppers entering the shop. "Thank you," trailed behind him.

"Anytime," she said to the retreating doctor. *And in the meantime, I'll be praying for that miracle. And a well-qualified intern*, Joy thought as she watched the doctor depart the building.

Between assisting the shoppers and answering phone calls for floral orders for patients, Joy barely noticed that the morning had passed. "It's a pity my part-time assistant's position is on hold thanks to budget constraints," she muttered, using the words that HR had sent in the email she received a week ago. "Oh well. Maybe I can find myself another volunteer."

When Evelyn called and began a lengthy apology, Joy glanced up at the clock. Almost noon. Where had the time gone?

"So I promise, next time I'll be there," Evelyn continued. "But there was this absolutely adorable little girl who was just admitted, and her mama was having a bit of trouble getting her to settle down, so I found some children's books, and the next thing I knew I had missed our coffee and a whole lot of other things I should have been doing."

"Relax," Joy said. "I only just now noticed the time."

"So you wouldn't have been there either?" Evelyn laughed. "We are a fine pair, aren't we?"

"I'm glad you called." Joy glanced around the shop to make sure it was empty before slipping into the back room. "I've got a prayer request. Dr. Barnhardt needs a miracle and an intern. Actually, a *well-qualified* intern," she corrected.

"I see." There was a long pause, and then Evelyn said, "Did he ask you to pray for that?"

"He did. Using those exact words." The bell rang on the door, alerting Joy to incoming shoppers. "Sorry, gotta go. I've got a customer."

"Okay," Evelyn said. "I can't wait to see what God does with this."

"Neither can I," Joy agreed. "I have a feeling it'll be something good."

The remainder of the day flew by, and the next thing Joy knew, she was locking up the shop. She loved her job, and she especially loved those days when time slipped away and then returned to surprise her hours later.

Shrugging her purse over her shoulder, she crossed the now-empty lobby and stepped out into a glorious Charleston afternoon. Her phone buzzed in her purse, likely a text from her daughter, Sabrina, asking how her day at work had gone.

She retrieved her phone and texted Sabrina back. Moving to Charleston had certainly been the right decision. With her daughter and grandchildren nearby, her life was full even if a big part of her heart was still aching over the loss of her husband.

Joy spent the evening quietly puttering in her garden until the lack of light forced her to go inside. As she went about her nightly routine of dinner and bedtime with a favorite book and some television in between, she once again prayed for Dr. Barnhardt. He would have his miracle, of this she was certain.

The next morning, Joy awakened surer of Dr. Barnhardt's soon-to-come miracle than ever. As she passed Rainbow Row, she suddenly remembered the dollhouse her father had made for her sixth birthday. He'd painted it that exact shade of pink. Deep in thought, she arrived at the hospital and was startled to find the parking lot blocked and yellow crime scene tape across the path she always took to the angel. "What's happening?" she asked an officer stationed nearby once she'd made her way to him.

He waved his hand behind him as his radio squawked. "The angel is gone."

Chapter Two

"The angel statue is gone?" Joy's heart lurched. Then she shook her head. "Impossible!"

"Tell that to my boss," he said, giving her a look that said he had no patience for this line of questioning. The tall, thin policeman with a clipboard under his arm scrutinized her. The nameplate over his pocket said Williams, J.

"Who are you?" he demanded.

"Joy Atkins," she said, clutching her bundle of blooms as she looked around and then back at the officer. "I run the gift shop here at the hospital. And I walk by Mercy—the statue—every day. I declare, I can't imagine that someone just took her. I mean, how could they, for goodness' sake? She's a heavy, life-size statue on a pedestal beside a very busy hospital."

Officer Williams held out the clipboard and then reached for the pen in his pocket. "Did you see anything, Mrs. Atkins?"

"Heavens, how could I? I haven't been over there," she said. "You saw which direction I was walking when I came toward you. All I've laid eyes on are flashing lights, police officers, and crime scene tape."

He looked at her over wire-rimmed glasses. "So the answer is no."

"No, sir," she echoed. "I mean yes, sir, the answer is no."

"When were you last at the hospital?"

"Yesterday afternoon," she said. "I closed up the gift shop around three and then walked down Tradd Street that way to go home." She gestured behind her to indicate the direction of her normal route.

"And was there a flower on the statue's base at that time?" Officer Williams asked.

"I don't know," Joy said. "I didn't go by her on the way home. But sometimes there's a flower there—a Noisette."

"A Noisette?" The officer looked very confused, his pen in midair over the pad.

"Sorry, I'm a bit of a rosarian. A Noisette is a type of rose. Is there one there this morning?"

He ignored her question. "When was the last time you saw one? And did you see who put it there?"

"Probably two weeks ago," she said. "And no, sir, I've never seen the person put the rose there. I figure they must do it at night. Did you find another one today?"

"Yes, a rose was found where the statue used to be. Unless forensics removed it already, it should be there." Officer Williams eyed her curiously. "Why do you say they put it there at night if you've never seen anyone do it?"

"Oh," Joy said. "Well, simple. I get here early, usually before seven. I was a little late today. I had a call from my granddaughter, and that put me a little behind schedule. But you know how it is with grandchildren. When they're chatty, you just have to ..." She trailed off.

The officer tilted his head. "So how does that figure into your theory that whoever is putting that flower on the statue is doing it at night?"

"Because when the rose is there on my morning walk in, it's never wilted. I figure that whoever places the rose on the statue must do it within a few hours at most of when I see it. A rose doesn't do well off the bush unless it's kept in water."

Officer Williams wrote something down then looked up at Joy. "So you're usually walking by at what, six forty-five, give or take a few minutes?"

"Yes, sir. Thereabouts," she said. "I set the timer to have the coffeepot on before the seven a.m. shift starts. It starts brewing at six forty-five then remains on warm until we use it up. The nurses and doctors appreciate it, and I am an early riser regardless."

He nodded and went back to his writing. "And you're saying the flower is just a few hours past having been taken out of water?"

"Oh yes. No more than that."

"Because it isn't wilted."

A statement, not a question. Still Joy nodded. "Yes, sir, that's right."

"Anything else you can tell me, Mrs. Atkins?" He glanced up again. "Any suspicious persons that you've seen hanging around? Maybe threats you've overheard? People talking about putting a rose on the statue?"

"Threats? Oh no. People who come into the gift shop are generally either very kind or very quiet. The quiet ones are usually worried about a loved one who's a patient here. I find that out over coffee or a discussion about gardening. Something like that."

Joy paused. "Of course, not all of them open up to me, but some do."

"Right. So," Officer Williams said on an exhale of breath. "So no threats. And no talk of putting roses on the statue." He looked down at the bundle of flowers in her hand. "No one buying a similar rose from you. Or you bringing one to place there?"

Joy frowned. "Excuse me, Officer, but that's ridiculous. If I put a rose there, wouldn't I have said so?" She shook her head. "A Noisette rose like that can't be purchased in my shop, so that's not possible either."

His brows rose. "Why can't it?"

"Because I've never seen one like it. It's been a mystery to me for a while as to what kind it is. I've researched to see if I could place it, but so far, I haven't found another example of it online. I'm just a hobbyist, so an expert rosarian might not be surprised to see a Noisette rose with that coloring, but I certainly am."

The officer took a few more notes. "Anything else you can add to this?"

"No, I can't think of anything," she said. "Except that I'm very sad she's gone, and I hope y'all find her soon."

Officer Williams lowered his clipboard and put his pen in his shirt pocket. His gaze moved from her face to the bundle in her arms. "How can you be reached if the detectives have more questions?"

"As I said, I manage the gift shop. I'll be there until three, maybe later depending on whether we have customers or not."

"And a contact number besides your place of business?"

Joy gave the police officer her cell phone number. "You can always come by the shop too."

"Duly noted," he said dryly, though he didn't write it down.

"Well," she said as brightly as she could manage, "if that's all, I'll just get on in to work then."

"Go ahead but take care that you don't get behind the crime scene tape."

With a nod to the officer, she set off down the sidewalk. As she stepped around the trees that shaded the pathway, Joy stuttered to a stop.

There behind the crime scene tape was a void where the Angel of Mercy had stood guard over the hospital for more than one hundred and fifty years—likely much more than that—and now she was gone.

"Unbelievable!"

"Exactly what I was thinking." Joy turned to see that Anne Mabry had joined her on the sidewalk.

With her warm laughter and her penchant for exercising her gift for Southern hospitality whenever she could, Anne's job as a hospital volunteer suited her. Her husband, Ralph, had recently retired from the pastorate and was serving as the hospital chaplain, which was another reason she loved her work.

Only this morning she wasn't laughing. And for good reason.

Instead, Anne's lovely smile had been replaced with a look of disbelief that likely matched her own. "Good night, nurse! I just can't believe it's gone," she said as she tucked a strand of hair behind her ear. "I sometimes go see her on my break, and now she just … oh, that flower is here again."

"Noisette rose," Joy said, "and a rare one. I've never seen a red center on a Noisette of any kind. And it isn't wilted, so it's only been here for a few hours at most."

Anne shook her head. "Seriously, Joy. I'm just beside myself. Who would do such a thing? The angel has stood in place for more than a century!"

Joy looked past Anne to see Evelyn hurrying toward them.

"What's going on around here?" Evelyn demanded when she reached them. "There are policemen all over. I couldn't even park in the garage without—" She stopped short and placed her hand over her mouth. "Oh." She shook her head. "Oh," she said again. "It's gone."

Then her eyes narrowed. Her shoulders straightened.

"Well that's just not right," she said. A stickler for order and protocol as well as a history buff, the head of the hospital records department was clearly indignant at the travesty that had befallen the hospital. "Someone's got to do something about this!"

Joy nodded to the side. "I spoke to a policeman over yonder named Officer Williams. He took my statement." She glanced at Anne then back to Evelyn. "If either of you saw something you thought was important, I'm sure he'd take your statements too."

"I don't know what I would have to say," Anne said. "I'm just flabbergasted." She let out a quick chuckle that held no humor. "I guess I've already made that clear."

Joy looked toward the entrance of the hospital. "How about we talk about it over coffee?"

She led the way to the front entrance and into the lobby. Unlike the normal hushed atmosphere at this time of the morning, the space was filled with activity.

Two men and a woman in dark trousers, white shirts, and police badges hanging from around their necks on silver chains—

obviously police detectives—were huddled together near the eleva-tors. All three looked up as Joy and her friends approached.

"Just opening the gift shop," Joy called out as she jammed her keys into the lock of the gift shop door. "I have coffee ready if y'all would like some."

"Thank you." The female detective, a tall woman with dark hair and only the slightest bit of silver at her temples, smiled. "We're fine for now."

A moment later, her expression changed. She leaned in to the other detectives and said something then walked toward the ladies. "I assume at least one of you works here."

All three nodded. "Yes, ma'am, that's right," Evelyn said. "I'm in the records department, Joy Atkins runs the gift shop, and Anne Mabry is a volunteer. My name is Evelyn Perry."

"Detective Rebekah Osborne, Charleston PD. Pleased to meet you all. Obviously, you couldn't miss the fact that the Angel of Mercy statue is missing. Have any of you spoken with a police officer about what happened?"

"I have," Joy volunteered as she jangled her keys in the lock and then swung the door to the gift shop open. "On my way in I was interviewed by Officer Williams."

"Officer Williams." Detective Osborne retrieved a small note-book from her jacket pocket and made a note. Then she looked up. "And you are Joy Atkins, manager of the hospital gift shop."

Joy tucked her keys into her pocket. "That's right. Come on in. I've got fresh coffee already brewed."

She turned on the lights with her free hand, being careful not to jostle the flowers she still held tucked under her other arm. "The pot is in the back. I'll just put these flowers in the sink back here and be with you in a minute."

"All right," the detective called.

When Joy returned with a tray holding three steaming mugs of coffee, she found Detective Osborne at the front counter deep in conversation with Evelyn while Anne nodded and interjected the occasional statement of her own.

"Coffee is ready." She placed the tray on the counter. "I know how Evelyn and Anne like their coffees, but I didn't think to ask you, Detective."

"Black is fine," she said. "And thank you."

Joy retrieved the cup with no added sugar or creamer and handed it to Detective Osborne. "Give me just a sec, and I'll go grab mine. I should probably get a bigger tray, but we rarely have more than one or two at a time who want my coffee." She made a quick trip to the back room and filled her favorite mug, decorated with wildflowers, then returned to the group.

The detective was taking a sip from her mug. "It's excellent coffee, Mrs. Atkins. I can't imagine why there's not a line out the door. Is this a local blend?"

"Thank you. And no, it isn't. Before I moved to Charleston, I lived in Houston. There was a lovely man named Raphael who owned a coffee shop near me. When the requests started coming in for take-home versions of the coffee he was selling there, Raphael started bagging and selling his own coffee beans. Lucky for me, when I moved here to live closer to family, the company had become large enough to include shipping in their business plan."

The detective took another sip and smiled. "It's delicious. Do they sell it in Charleston?"

"I'm afraid not. I order for myself and get enough to supply the gift shop too." She nodded across the lobby. "If they plan on lingering, most folks get their coffee over at the coffee shop, so I don't require a large quantity here."

Detective Osborne took one more sip and then set her mug down. "Before we go any further, I will need the name of that company. I've got to get some of this."

Joy repeated the information she had given out to countless gift shop customers already. Then she chuckled. "I've told Raphael that he needs to send a stack of business cards with my next order. He probably gets a lot of sales through this shop."

"For good reason." The detective wrote down the name of Raphael's company then sobered. "Thank you. Now, back to the missing statue. I'll get Officer Williams's notes, but is there anything you'd like to add to what you told him?"

Evelyn shrugged. "This is probably completely unrelated, but there was that guy who kept skateboarding around the statue a couple of weeks ago. Remember him?" she asked Joy and Anne. "Norm tried so hard to catch him."

"I do," Joy said. "Poor Norm. He skinned both knees and nearly broke his arm the last time he made the attempt."

"Norm?"

"Norm Ashford," Anne said. "He's one of our security guards. He generally works the night or evening shift. He's complained about a skateboarder coming up at night and trying to skate around the statue."

"Recently?" she asked Anne.

"Well, I don't know exactly, but he did mention it to me a few days ago in passing. We were talking about how difficult it is to keep kids from trampling the flowers or climbing on the statue. He said he'd caught someone standing on the statue base in the middle of the night. Said it was the strangest thing. The person was dressed all in black—long black pants and a black sweatshirt with the hood up—in this heat! When he walked up, they took off. I didn't think to ask when it was, but it had to be at least a week ago that he told me about it."

"Okay, thank you. I'll check with Mr. Ashford about that, but there's nothing unusual about a kid skateboarding on public property. Unfortunately, we deal with that a lot. They're usually harmless, but because these guys tend to skate in groups and video themselves trying—and usually failing—to defy gravity, we get calls to handle them. I should add, though, that they're generally skating where they shouldn't be skating, so there's that."

"I don't think that guy was one of them," Evelyn said.

"Why do you think this?" the detective asked her.

"Well, if he's the same guy I'm thinking of—and how many guys dressed like that in Charleston in June are there?—he wasn't with anyone else, and he certainly wasn't a kid."

Detective Osborne paused in her note taking to look up at Evelyn. "How do you know?"

"Because I saw a skateboarder dressed like that a while ago too. My husband was away at a conference a couple of weekends ago, so I thought I'd spend some time organizing the storage room where the old hospital records are kept. I'm something of a night owl, and

I never can get anything extra like that done when my staff is here." Evelyn paused. "I was just finishing up when I heard this odd sound."

"What kind of odd sound?" the detective asked.

"A swooshing sound. Like wheels but nothing like the noise a cart or a gurney makes. I heard it again, so I went out into the hall and a skateboarder nearly ran me down. I guess he was going up and down the hall."

"He," the detective repeated as she went back to her notes. "A man."

"Yes indeed, a man." Evelyn nodded emphatically. "I couldn't see much of his face because of the hood and his sunglasses, but I saw that he had a full beard. He was wearing all black from the shoes on his feet to the hood covering his head. And he had one of those cameras strapped to the front of him." She chuckled. "I yelled at him when he passed me, and he just about fell off his skateboard. I think I startled him more than he did me. He jumped off his board, grabbed it, and ran for the stairwell. By the time I got to the stairs, he was long gone."

"Dressed in black like the guy standing on the statue," the detective observed.

"Yes," Evelyn said. "Do you think he could be a suspect?"

"At the beginning of a case, everyone's a suspect until someone proves they're not."

Chapter Three

THE DETECTIVE WROTE A FEW more lines in her notebook then returned her attention to Evelyn. "Okay. What did the board look like? Can you remember anything about it? Color, length? Any detail would be helpful."

"Well," she said slowly, "I don't remember anything specific about the top of the skateboard, but I do recall that the wheels were yellow."

Detective Osborne nodded and made another note. "Did you tell security about what you saw?"

"Yes," Evelyn said. "I called the security office Monday morning and told the guy who answered the phone about it. I think he just chalked it up to a visitor taking advantage of a long hall late at night." She chuckled. "Believe me, it's not the strangest thing a visitor has ever done."

The detective scribbled some more on her notepad, allowing silence to fall between them. Finally she looked up.

"I think I've got what I need for now. Is there anything else that any of you would like to add?" When Anne shook her head, she turned her attention to Evelyn. "What about you, Mrs. Perry? Other than the mystery skateboarder, do you have any insights?"

Evelyn frowned. "Well, we did have a patient recently that might be of interest. HIPAA laws won't let me divulge his name, but I can

say he had quite an unsavory reputation. He was here for an operation that required a lengthy stay—two weeks almost. The only
reason I mention him is because we had several police officers ask
for his records since he was here. One just yesterday."

Anne nodded. "I remember rumors circulating about that man.
But he was always very polite and kind to me. Nothing like the
criminal I'd heard he was. So perhaps he wasn't that kind of person
anymore. People do change."

Joy remembered the fellow Anne and Evelyn referred to very
well. Alan Parker came in under police escort, not a completely
unusual circumstance.

Often the emergency room was called upon to patch up a future
prisoner before he or she was delivered to the Charleston jail. But
Alan Parker was different.

The officers who guarded Parker during the time he was a
patient at Mercy Hospital were not members of the Charleston
police force. They wore serious expressions and dark clothing, and
the guns strapped beneath their coats were impossible to miss. So
were the black Suburbans posted at the front and back exits of
the building.

No, there was something very different about Alan Parker.

"Okay, so if I am understanding you," Detective Osborne said,
"you had a high-profile patient recently. Would you say it was three
weeks ago? More? Less?"

Evelyn gave her a doubtful look. "As supervisor of records,
I don't think it's appropriate to be that specific. Let's say he was
recently here and leave it at that. I'm sure you understand we would
tell you more if we could."

Both Anne and Joy nodded.

"Yes, I understand," Detective Osborne said. "And I'm sure I can get clearance to find out what I need to. If I do, I'll come back with a subpoena so we can do this the right way."

Evelyn smiled. "I'll help however I can as long as you show me a subpoena."

Detective Osborne closed her notepad. "I'll do that, and no hard feelings. You have your job to do, and I respect that." She took another quick sip of coffee and then put the mug down to retrieve three business cards from her pocket. "You ladies have been helpful. If you remember anything else, would you call me?"

Joy looked down at the card and then back up at the police officer. "We will, of course. I hope you bring her back soon. I miss her already."

"We're going to try." The detective put away her notebook and pen. "I'm done here. Mrs. Atkins, I prefer you keep the gift shop closed to customers until the officer in charge gives you the all clear. Until then we're in an active investigation zone."

"Yes, all right," Joy said. "I'm sure I'll have phone orders for deliveries to patients. Is it okay for me to fill those orders and make those deliveries?"

"That should be fine. Just try as much as possible to stay in one place and be available to any of the officers who might need to ask follow-up questions."

Norm Ashford, the elderly security guard who had been with the hospital since he retired from the Charleston Police Department, stuck his head into the gift shop.

"Hi, Norm," Joy greeted him.

Norm grinned at her and said, "Detective Osborne, you're needed out here."

The detective stood. "Are you Norm Ashford? The man who saw someone standing on the statue recently?"

"That's me. I gave my statement already, though," he said.

"I'd still like to talk to you if you've got a minute."

"Yes, ma'am." He waved at the ladies then held the door open so Detective Osborne could exit the shop. Then, with a tip of his cap, Norm followed her down the hall.

Joy exhaled. "Well, this has been quite the beginning to our day, hasn't it, ladies?"

"Oh, look at the time," Anne exclaimed. "I need to get upstairs and check in."

After Anne left, Evelyn turned to Joy. "I never gave that skateboarder another thought after I called security. Now I wonder if I was almost run down by the thief who took the Angel of Mercy. I should have insisted the security office look into the incident."

"Think of it this way," Joy said. "You were able to give a description."

"Not good enough," Evelyn said. "I didn't see his face, and all I got off the skateboard was that it had yellow wheels."

"Which may be all Detective Osborne needs to find him."

"What is this world coming to?" a familiar voice called. "Anne told me I would find you all in here."

Joy looked in the direction of the approaching voice and spied Nurse Shirley Bashore walking toward them. While Evelyn and Anne were longtime residents of Charleston, Shirley had only resided in the city for two months. She'd made the move in order to better see to the care of her mother, who had also been a nurse until the early effects of a serious health issue made working impossible.

Joy's grin was swift. "Good morning, Shirley. Evelyn and I were just wondering the same thing."

Shirley shook her head and smoothed a wayward strand of hair into her pulled-back style. "How is it that statue stood there for over a century and no one messed with her until now? And of all things, someone took her while I was on duty."

While waiting for a permanent spot on the day shift, Shirley had become a floater who worked in whatever unit she was needed. With a mother who needed her at home, Joy knew that Shirley was grateful for the work, though too often she ended up on the night shift.

"The police have been crawling all over the place," Evelyn said.

"You wouldn't know it up in maternity. It must be a full moon, because we've been so busy I barely remember taking a break all night." She paused. "Have you heard if the police have any leads?"

"If they do, they're not saying," Evelyn said. "I'm sorry to do this, but I need to get to my office. I've got a phone meeting scheduled in a half hour, and I need to prepare for it. If either of you hear anything, would you let me know?"

Joy nodded. "Of course."

"Much as I wish I could say yes to that, I'm headed home," Shirley said as she waved goodbye to Evelyn. "The senior bus will have picked Mama up for her breakfast and bingo outing over at the center, so I'll have the house to myself for a few hours. I've got laundry and housecleaning to do before I can think about getting some sleep."

"I've been told to keep the gift shop closed until the officer in charge allows me to open again, so unless you're anxious to get started on that laundry and housecleaning, come in and have some coffee and a chat first, Shirley," Joy suggested. "I've got a stash of decaf I can brew for you."

"Oh honey," Shirley said with a hearty chuckle, "I don't have to hurry. I'll take the chat, but don't even try to serve me that nasty decaf." She retrieved a lime-green water bottle emblazoned with I AM THE LORD'S FAVORITE in rhinestones from her bag and showed it to Joy. "I'm trying to drink more water, although I have to admit it doesn't taste near as good as cream soda."

Joy leaned toward her. "I'm with you on the decaf, though I'd prefer water to cream soda any day."

"That's why you're so trim, Joy," Shirley said with a chuckle. "As soon as the Lord decides that fresh bread and butter is a vegetable, I will be the happiest of all His children. In the meantime, I'm just going to manage."

"You manage quite well, it seems to me," Joy told her. "Now come on. Let's chat before you go home. I'd like to get to know you better."

Shirley followed her into the back of the gift shop, where she sat on one of the two chairs on either side of the small table that was used for everything from taking breaks to tallying up inventory and marking prices on items for sale in the store.

"How are you settling in?" Joy asked her once she'd claimed her favorite wildflower-bedecked coffee mug and poured herself a cup. "I know it wasn't easy making the decision to move here, but I'm sure your mother appreciates that you've done this."

"Well, Mama and I have our moments, but we've mostly learned how to live under the same roof again. Still, I think the decision to move was easier than the decision to stay once I got here."

"I wish I didn't understand, but I do," Joy said. "I guess the idea of what you're headed toward propels you, but once you're here you're faced with how to live with your new normal."

"It's hard, isn't it? You want to be there for the one you love, but what you think it's going to be like isn't necessarily what it turns out to be." Shirley's expression softened as her brown eyes focused on her hands now resting on the tabletop. "This isn't easy to admit, me being a nurse and all, but I'm having a hard time with her. I can tell her what to do when she has one of her spells, but whether she does it or not depends on her mood and not because she believes I know what I'm talking about. To my mama I will forever be her child and not a grown woman with a nursing degree and plenty of years of experience."

Joy took a sip of her coffee. "She's your mother, and she's used to being the one in charge."

"I know you're right," Shirley said, "but I want the best for her, and I sure don't mean to let her boss me around when her health is at risk." She let out a sigh. "I love her, and I'm going to keep doing what I'm doing. As sassy as I am, well, you can imagine who I got it from." She paused to laugh, and Joy joined her. "Somehow the Lord will show us the way. Of that I'm sure."

"Yes, He will." Joy took another sip of coffee and returned her mug to the table.

"You seem like you made an easy transition, Joy," Shirley said. "I know you love your family, but tell me the truth. Are you sorry you moved here?"

"No," Joy said slowly, "but I don't know that I would say it's been easy. I'm thrilled for the time I get to spend with my daughter and grandbabies, but it's a completely different life than the one I lived in Houston. There's so much I miss," she admitted. "But now it seems like an eternity ago."

"Oh, honey, I'm sorry. I wasn't thinking. Of course you miss your husband."

"Yes, that's true," Joy said. "And if wishes would bring him back, he'd be here right now. But the Lord called him home, and there's no changing that. I've made peace with it." She paused. "You know what I'm struggling with, though?"

"What's that?"

She shrugged. "It's going to sound silly. I'm a grown woman. I shouldn't feel this way, but I still feel a little bit adrift. I'm not unhappy, but I haven't quite settled into my place yet. I had so many irons in the fire in Houston, but that's really not the case here."

"Joy," Shirley said slowly, "I could talk to you the rest of the morning about how I see that you fit in here at the hospital, but you feel the way you feel, and that's that. Just like I plan to ask the Lord to give me a job that doesn't change from day to day, I'm going to ask Him to heal that feeling in you. Is that too bold?"

She grinned. "Not at all. I'm a big fan of bold prayers."

"I'm glad you think so. Mama raised me to be bold in my faith." Shirley shook her head. "Enough of that. Catch me up on the scoop about the theft."

Once Shirley was up to speed on the details, she sat back in her chair and shook her head. "And to think all of that happened while I was right here in the hospital."

Joy nodded. "It certainly looks that way."

Shirley's expression grew determined. "You know what? I might not have had time to take a break last night, but I know some folks did. I wonder if I ought to ask around and see if anyone saw anything out of the ordinary."

Joy perked up. "It couldn't hurt. Something that seemed normal at the time may look suspicious now that people know what was happening to the statue overnight. I've got Detective Osborne's card. Would you like the information?"

"Show it to me, and I'll take a picture."

Joy retrieved the card and set it on the table. Shirley snapped a photo.

Joy noticed a look of concern on Shirley's face. "Is something wrong?"

"Something you just said has made me think. There was something normal that happened, but now that I think about it, I may need to follow up on it." She reached for her phone and tucked it into her pocket. "I'm not ready to call the police yet, but I might, depending on what I find out when I come back to work tonight."

A bell dinged, alerting Joy to someone's arrival in the store. She rose and peered around the corner to see Officer Williams standing there.

"You're free to open now, ma'am," he said then ducked back out the door.

"Thank you," Joy called before the door shut completely.

Joy turned back to Shirley, who gathered up her purse and stood.

"That's my cue to say goodbye." Shirley reached over to give Joy a hug. "Everything's going to be fine, you know."

Joy grinned. "I was about to tell you that."

"We're a fine pair." Shirley's expression sobered. "You know what might help you, Joy? I see all these beautiful flowers here, and I know you've got a talent for gardening. Have you thought about joining a garden club or something like that? Mama used to belong to the local one. She loved it."

Joy groaned. "Have you been reading my emails?"

"Not lately," Shirley said with a chuckle. "Why?"

"Suffice it to say, you're not the first one to come up with that idea." Joy shrugged. "My neighbor is the current president of the local group. When I first moved in, she tried to convince me to join."

"Why didn't you?"

"I was busy unpacking at the time, and it seemed like more than I could manage." She shrugged again. "I know. I've been here six months. She's invited me to six monthly meetings, and I've turned her down every time."

"Doesn't sound like unpacking is your excuse." Shirley appeared to study Joy for a moment. "Maybe the truth is you just need a tiny kick in the pants."

Chapter Four

THAT EVENING, AFTER FORTIFYING HERSELF with an extra scoop of ice cream, Joy got online and looked for the website of the garden club her neighbor kept urging her to join. After a few wrong clicks, she finally found it. "'Petals and Plants,'" she read out loud. "'Charleston's up-and-coming garden club for green thumbs of all shapes and sizes.'"

Hmm. Interesting. This Saturday's meeting featured an expert on the Noisette rose. What were the odds? Maybe Shirley was right. Maybe this was her "tiny kick in the pants."

The next morning, Joy was still pondering Shirley's comment about avoiding the garden club when the gift shop door opened. Because the police had redirected all deliveries from yesterday to today, her usual Wednesday morning restocking was happening on Thursday.

She'd been at it for almost an hour, with a volunteer working the cash register until just a few minutes ago, so Joy was grateful to straighten and stretch her back. Though she loved working at the gift shop, unpacking boxes was not her favorite chore.

While she could have the volunteer do that, she preferred seeing to the task herself. That way she could deal with any delivery issues immediately and not risk putting broken merchandise out for sale.

"I'll be right with you," Joy called out. She tucked a handful of books among the half dozen boxes that remained from the morning's delivery, and then she hurried out into the shop. "Please do browse and let me know if ..."

Her mouth opened but words escaped her. There standing before her was the exact image of the missing statue. To be certain, this was no stone maiden, nor were her clothes the old-fashioned garments that the angel wore. But that smile, those eyes. That expression. It was her.

But not her.

She couldn't be. And yet she looked just like her.

Joy shook her head when she realized she was staring at the young woman who could be a twin to the missing stone angel. "I'm sorry. Can I help you?"

"I hope so. I'm Angela Simpson. Today's my first day." She shrugged, and the heart-shaped gold locket and a small key hanging from her neck caught the light. "I saw Dr. Barnhardt in the hallway. He sent me to the HR department to do some paperwork, but I'm not sure where to find it."

Joy gathered her wits. "I can get you where you need to be. Human Resources is on the second floor. You can take the elevators, over there, or use the stairs, which are just across the hall. First door on the left after you get off the elevator."

"Thank you." Her smile rose. "I do appreciate the help."

"Anytime," Joy said, trying not to stare but failing miserably. "If you like coffee, I've always got some perking and love to share. And to chat."

"I like chatting too. I'll look forward to it." Angela paused. "Thank you."

And then she winked.

The action, so familiar, took Joy aback. It had been what she'd half expected from the statue but never something she would have thought an intern would offer.

"Sorry," Angela said, cringing. "Did I offend you? I wink. I know. I don't mean to be rude."

"No, it's fine," Joy said. "It was just ... unexpected," she managed. "I'm glad you're here. You're quite literally an answer to prayer. Are you from Charleston? Is that how you ended up here?"

The dark-haired beauty's cheerful expression slipped. Obviously, she felt some measure of discomfort in Joy's questions.

"I'm sorry. I tend to be nosy," Joy quickly amended.

"No, it's fine, really."

"I'm very glad to see you. Please tell Dr. Barnhardt that I had no doubt he would get an answer."

"I will," she said. "Although I'm not sure how soon I will see him. Does he come into the gift shop much?"

"Only when the coffee is fresh," Joy said.

Angela walked a few steps toward the door then turned back to look at her. "So it's a big deal that the statue is missing. She must be valuable."

A statement, not a question. "Very." Joy gave her a brief explanation of the angel's value to Mercy Hospital.

"Right, but I was thinking how much she was worth." She shrugged. "You, know, financially. Like out there on the black market. Someone must have thought they could make some money off her."

"Oh goodness," Joy said. "I hadn't even thought of that. But I'm sure the police are doing their best to find her, and they will." She paused. "Soon."

"Of course. Now tell me again, where is HR exactly?"

After reminding Angela of the directions, Joy sent her on her way with a repeated invitation to come have a cup of coffee anytime. As the young woman hurried from the shop, she nearly ran into Garrison Baker, Mercy Hospital's new administrator.

Joy smiled as she looked through the gift shop's glass door to see Garrison sidestep the energetic intern. He caught Joy looking and smiled back. She had anticipated his entrance into the gift shop by slipping back to pour a mug for him. Two sugar cubes and a dash of creamer was his preferred combination.

Garrison's predecessor, Henry Sanchez, was the man who had convinced Joy to accept the job of managing the gift shop.

She'd mentioned to Dr. Amanda Taylor, her daughter Sabrina's best friend, that she was looking for volunteer work. The last thing Joy wanted was an actual job, but rather just something to take up the time she found she had far too much of. Amanda had promised to speak to her boss, the hospital administrator.

Apparently, Amanda talked up Joy's skills to the point that Henry had hired her on the spot. After just a few weeks of her volunteering, he had cajoled Joy into taking on the project of whipping the gift shop into shape.

Joy had been reluctant. The gift shop hadn't been properly run for years. Instead, a series of volunteers opened the shop when they could manage it and rarely ordered more than the basic necessities when the shelves began to look thin.

However, with absolutely no experience running a store but plenty of experience running a home, Joy had agreed and found that she'd taken on a huge challenge. To her surprise, she loved every minute of turning the sad old gift shop into a place where the coffeepot was always on and the flowers were not only appreciated but sold out every day.

When Henry retired, he came by the shop to let her know he'd hired Garrison on the condition that he'd keep the budget and the manager of the gift shop unchanged.

Garrison opened the gift shop door and stepped inside. "Good morning, Joy. I smell coffee."

Joy set Garrison's coffee mug on the counter. "You know I've got to keep the boss happy. I wouldn't want to get fired for having bad coffee," she said with a chuckle.

"I'll get fired long before you, Joy." He paused to take a sip and then smiled. "Anyone who makes coffee this good and has managed to turn this shop around so well probably ought to have my job anyway."

"Thank you," she said. "But I think your job is safe. Speaking of jobs, I thought the hospital was in a hiring freeze."

He took another sip then seemed to be studying his mug a moment before looking back up at Joy. "Unfortunately, we are. I've got to get a budget increase past the board, which won't be easy since there are a lot of things here that need fixing. You know that from the condition you found the gift shop, or at least that's what I've heard."

"It was a mess," Joy said. "But that wasn't anyone's fault, really. There just hadn't been anyone willing to take on the job of organizing and running it in a long time. Volunteers can only do so much."

"Agreed, and you have to have a budget, which you really didn't. Henry told me how you did most of the work using your own money and then wouldn't let him reimburse you."

Joy waved away the statement. "It was a labor of love, and I wasn't the only one."

"Well, with a bigger budget I can just imagine what we could get done here. But things like updating and maintaining the security system and more staff come before that. My priority is to give the patients the best quality medical care we can provide. Then comes everything else. And since I promised Henry I wouldn't cut anything, I mean to keep that promise."

"The gift shop is doing fine and paying for itself now, I would imagine. Don't you worry about us. Whoever put the idea in the suggestion box to have a donation station at the counter was a genius. I wish I'd thought of it. We take in at least a hundred dollars every week just by people putting in their change or sometimes making larger donations." She paused. "Back to the hiring freeze. So no one can be hired at all?"

Garrison shook his head. "Not until the new budget is approved by the board. Why?"

"That intern who nearly ran you down? She said she just got hired."

One dark brow lifted. "That's not exactly right."

"Oh. Well, maybe I misunderstood, but she was clear about having just been hired."

"She has. I thought I emailed you." Garrison shrugged. "Maybe that's still on my secretary's very lengthy to-do list. Angela is your new assistant."

"Mine?" She stared at him. "Why? The volunteers and I do well enough. Couldn't the funds be used elsewhere?"

"They could, but this was a specific grant. Funds were earmarked for a part-time assistant for your gift shop, Joy. Angela was chosen. I'm sorry I didn't get to involve you in the process, but she came as part of the deal."

Joy shook her head. "So someone paid the hospital to hire Angela?"

Garrison frowned. "I'd rather say that someone provided a nice donation and suggested Angela for the position that donation created. Her references were checked, and she was given the job. In my defense, it all happened very quickly. I apologize for not giving you fair warning."

"No, it's fine. She seems very sweet, and I'm more than grateful for the extra help." Joy paused. "Did you notice she looks familiar?"

Garrison nodded. "I did. Couldn't put my finger on it."

"She is a carbon copy of the Angel of Mercy. Well, not in her clothing choice, of course, but she could have posed for the statue's face when it was created."

"To tell you the truth, I was so busy trying not to get run over by her that I didn't pay much attention to her face. I didn't realize that was her until you told me you'd met the new hire."

The security guard walked past the gift shop window, sending Joy's thoughts in a slightly different direction. "I know it's barely been twenty-four hours, but I wonder if there have been any leads in the theft of the statue."

His congenial expression sobered. "I had a briefing with the police on my way to work this morning. I thought it best to make a call to them before I got started with my day. Anyway, they're exploring all leads." Garrison shrugged. "Or at least that's what the desk officer said who answered my call. I've got a meeting with the head detective at three to get an update."

"So they have leads," Joy said. "That sounds hopeful."

"I want to believe it is. Mercy Hospital just isn't the same without the Angel of Mercy." He paused. "If you believe in the legends, she watches over the hospital."

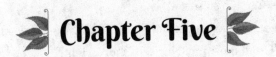

Chapter Five

"WELL, THE STORY ITSELF ISN'T a legend," Joy protested. "Evelyn Perry told me a massive fire swept through Charleston during the Civil War and much of the city was destroyed, as was most of the hospital. The wing closest to the Angel of Mercy was the only section that escaped total destruction. When the hospital was rebuilt in the late 1800s, the old wing's renovation was managed by the newly formed preservation society." Joy paused.

"People say," Garrison said, "that was the first miracle at Mercy Hospital."

"Well," Joy said slowly, "the first one that's survived history to be told. Evelyn might know of more. She's got records going way back into the hospital's history. She keeps saying she's going to organize those old records, but from what I understand she stays plenty busy with the new ones."

Garrison nodded. "So the bottom line is our angel needs to be returned."

"She does," Joy said. "If only someone had seen who took her. I guess that's too much to ask."

"Well, actually—"

The door burst open, and Shirley hurried in. "Joy, sometimes the Lord amazes me with how fast He works. My church prayer ladies were on it and so were we, but girl, you are never going to believe what just—" She stuttered to a stop when her gaze landed on Garrison. "Oh. I'm so sorry."

"I'm not," the administrator said, placing his coffee mug on the counter. "Good morning. Nurse Bashore, right?"

Shirley's surprised expression softened to the beginnings of a smile. "Good morning to you. And yes, I'm Shirley Bashore."

"You two haven't met?" Joy asked. "Let me remedy that. Shirley, this man runs the hospital and does a great job of it."

Garrison colored. "She's been paid to say that," he protested.

"Not true," Joy countered. "And Garrison, meet Shirley. She's an amazing nurse who just moved here from Atlanta two months ago."

"How have I not seen you around the hospital?" he asked.

"I've been working the night shift much of the time," Shirley explained. "Just biding my time until an opening comes up on the day shift. So my guess is we usually aren't in the building at the same time."

"You mentioned your church ladies," Garrison said. "What church do you attend, if you don't mind me asking?"

"Charleston AME on Calhoun Street," she said.

"Ah yes, Mother Emmanuel. Beautiful historic church. Over two hundred years old, isn't it?" At Shirley's nod, he continued. "I've heard good things about it. I'm still looking for a church home. It's hard to find a new place to worship when you loved the old one so much. But that's part of settling into a new city."

Shirley grinned. "You should try us out. I've only been attending a couple of months, and sometimes my work schedule interferes, but my mother has been attending since the sixties. They've been like a second family to her, especially after she lost my father three years ago."

"Good to know," he said. "I'll do that."

Silence fell between them.

"Yes, well maybe I'll see you there."

Garrison smiled. "I look forward to that."

Shirley met Joy's gaze then returned her attention to Garrison and shook her head. "Please, don't let me interrupt your conversation. I can call you later, Joy. After I've slept, that is. I got held over to help on the overnight shift, so I'm just leaving."

Garrison looked at his watch. "No, you stay, Nurse Bashore. I've got a couple of things to do before my next meeting." He glanced over at Joy. "Thanks for the coffee, Joy." His attention shifted to Shirley. "It's a pleasure to meet you. I hope I'll see you at church." He paused. "And perhaps around on the day shift soon."

"We've been praying for that," Joy told him.

"Then it's bound to happen." He bid them goodbye and left the shop.

Joy couldn't help noticing that her friend watched as the administrator disappeared from sight.

"He's a very nice man. A godly man," Joy amended. "And he's new to Charleston. Like you."

"He seems to be nice," Shirley said on an exhale of breath. "I'm a little embarrassed I barged in like that. I didn't see him standing there talking to you until I had already made a fool of myself."

"Shirley, you did not make a fool of yourself," Joy reassured her. "In fact, I got the impression that Garrison was very pleased to meet you. And I know he appreciated your suggestion of a possible church home."

Shirley shook her head. "Well anyway, as I was saying when I barged in here, can you believe how quickly God answered our prayers about the intern for Dr. Barnhardt? I was leaving the unit when I saw him talking with a young woman. She walked away as I got closer, and the doctor told me she's a new hire."

"It's a miracle," Joy said. "What with a hiring freeze on right now. However, she's not an intern."

"No?"

"No." Joy told her what Garrison had explained just a few minutes ago. "So it appears I'll have a part-time employee in the gift shop thanks to an anonymous donor." She paused. "I only wish they'd get the budget situation sorted out so the hiring freeze would be lifted."

"So do I," Shirley said. "That's why I'm stuck on the night shift, where there's a higher demand. There's also a need for day-shift nurses but no budget to pay for additional staff to fill the need. So I have to tell you, when I left the unit to head down here, I was praising the Lord for His swift answer for Dr. Barnhardt but just a little bit bothered He hadn't answered me as quickly. Oh my, that sounds selfish when I say it out loud, especially since I was wrong about the new hire being an intern."

"Not at all," Joy countered. "You'd like to be home and available for your mother at night."

"I would, though the sitter we got for her is working out just fine so far." She shrugged. "I guess He'll get to my request in His time not mine. But back to the new hire. Did you notice she looked familiar?"

"Did her face remind you of the Angel of Mercy statue too?" Joy asked.

Shirley nodded. "It's crazy how much she looks like her. I mean, we lose the stone angel and gain a real-life one."

"Whose name is Angela," Joy added.

"No."

She nodded. "Yes. Angela Simpson."

"Well, all right then. We got our angel back, sort of, and our prayers for help brought a miracle, only you got the help instead of Dr. Barnhardt. Why am I always surprised when the Lord shows me how creative He is?"

Joy waved Shirley to the table in the back and poured her a cup of coffee. "Were you able to speak to anyone who was on shift with you the night of the theft?"

"No. The person I needed to talk to was off last night." She glanced around as if checking to see whether they were alone and then returned her attention to Joy. "Here's what happened. One of the nurses in maternity disappeared for about an hour between two and three in the morning. No one knew where she went. Or, I'll put it this way. At least when the doctor asked for her, no one was willing to say they could find her."

"Oh. That sounds suspicious."

"It didn't at the time. Honestly, we all get tired, and it's not unusual to slip off and catch a little sleep when things are quiet. And it's also not unusual to cover for someone when a doctor is asking for them. I'm not saying we would tell a lie. I know I wouldn't. But I'm also not going to be quick to get someone in trouble."

"I understand. But things weren't quiet," Joy said. "I remember you telling us that you were extremely busy that night."

"We were," she said. "Exceptionally so."

"Did you notice how this nurse looked when she returned? Was she flushed, out of breath, anything like that?"

Shirley shook her head. "No, I was too busy to pay attention. I might not even have known she returned except that I overheard her talking to the charge nurse in the hall around three." She paused when two customers entered the shop. "I don't want to say more than that for now because I could be way off base in even thinking this is suspicious, you know?"

Joy rose to her feet. "Of course." She said goodbye to Shirley and went back to work. A half hour later Angela Simpson bounded into the gift shop to begin her first shift. She wore the same happy smile she'd had when Joy saw her earlier.

"I'm supposed to get with you to find out when you most need extra help in the shop. You're the one who'll set my hours, but I was told by HR to make sure you know that I'm budgeted for no more than twenty hours a week."

"Well," Joy said, "I am grateful for every one of those twenty hours I'll have help. If it's all right with you, I'd like to start you on an alternating four-hour schedule divided between morning and afternoon next week, but for today and tomorrow I want you with me in the mornings to train. Let's say eight o'clock until noon? Does that work for you?"

Angela's smile was swift and broad. "However I can best be of help," she said.

"Now let's get you situated and start your training. First, what do you know about making coffee?"

Angela was a quick learner, and by noon she was managing the cash register and charming the customers. Perhaps tomorrow Joy would allow her to try her hand at flower arranging. She would definitely put her on patient deliveries.

"You've been a delight," Joy told her. "I hope you've enjoyed today well enough to come back tomorrow."

Angela winked. "I wouldn't miss it. See you then, Mrs. A."

The next morning, Joy was in the middle of applying lipstick when she heard a WCHA reporter mention Mercy Hospital. "Sources say there was a high-level meeting between Charleston police detectives and Mercy Hospital administrator, Garrison Baker, yesterday afternoon."

Joy returned the makeup brush to the drawer and moved to a spot where she could see the television in her bedroom. Bailey Carver, the pretty brunette reporter who had interviewed Joy at the grand reopening of the gift shop several months ago, was standing in front of the ornate iron gates of Mercy Hospital. The empty base where the statue had once stood was impossible to miss behind her left shoulder.

Since the reporter was standing in daylight and it was not yet sunrise in Charleston this morning, the piece must have been shot yesterday afternoon or early evening. Joy settled on the edge of the bed to watch.

"The investigation is ongoing," Bailey continued, her expression conveying the seriousness of the situation. "Sources tell me that the police are being hampered by the fact that the security cameras that might have captured the theft were not working properly, and that the number of security guards on the property during the overnight hours was not sufficient to maintain a presence outside the building."

Garrison's words came to mind. *"Things like updating and maintaining the security system and more staff come before that."*

"Oh no," Joy whispered.

"I've walked these grounds myself," Bailey continued, "and there are no visible signs of that statue having been removed from the base you see behind me. No tire tracks, no footprints in the grass. Nothing to indicate how the beloved statue that has protected Mercy Hospital for a hundred and fifty years went missing. It's as if the Angel of Mercy just flew away without a trace." She paused. "Back to you, Kent."

At this point, the screen divided, and the morning news anchor appeared next to Bailey's remote feed. Kent Carpenter, who looked more like a California surfer than a Charleston reporter, wore a grim face.

"Bailey, I understand there is one clue that was left. A particular type of rose?" he said.

"Yes, Kent." She nodded for emphasis. "Apparently there was a rose left behind. The police are asking anyone who might have seen someone place a flower on the base of the statue—or maybe saw someone in the vicinity—during the overnight hours on Tuesday or the early morning of Wednesday to please speak up. They've asked that anyone with information call the number that is up on your screen."

Joy clicked off the television and rose to continue her morning routine. She felt terrible for Garrison. Surely he would be grilled regarding the broken cameras and lack of security personnel patrolling the grounds at night—if he hadn't been already.

With the news stations touting the lapses that led to the successful theft of the Angel of Mercy, Garrison might even lose his job. Joy frowned. Something needed to be done to help him. But what could she do? She was just the manager of the gift shop.

Joy finished her morning routine and, as was her custom, checked the weather before she left. Other than the possibility of light showers midday, it was going to be a lovely but warm summer day. A few minutes before six thirty she tucked her umbrella into her bag and set off for the hospital.

As she rounded the hospital and went toward the crime scene tape, Joy stuttered to a stop. There on the statue's empty base was a single Noisette rose. She moved closer, glancing around to see if anyone else was around.

Yes. There it was. A creamy Noisette rose with a center of scarlet that was only visible when you looked directly into the flower.

The Angel of Mercy rose.

Chapter Six

Joy glanced about, checking her surroundings once more. Other than light traffic on the street that ran alongside the hospital, there was no one around.

She reached out, retrieved the rose, and tucked it carefully into her bag. Once inside the gift shop, she placed the rose safely into a vase of water and set it beside the sink in the back room.

Now what?

Should she report it to the police? Joy gave that question a moment's thought before dialing.

Her call was answered on the second ring. "Osborne," a voice said. "How can I help you?"

"This is Joy Atkins, Detective Osborne. I work at the hospital gift shop. You gave me your card and told me I should call if I had any new information."

"Yes, of course," she said. "Joy with the great coffee. I've been exchanging emails with your roaster, Rafael. I can't wait to get my first shipment of beans. So, anyway, you've got some new information for me?"

"Not exactly new information, but I may have new evidence." Joy paused. "Someone left another rose on the statue's base last night. I found it this morning around six forty-five as I was coming in to work."

"Where is the rose now?" the detective asked.

"I've got it in a vase in the back of the store," Joy told her. "Just as with all the others that I've found, this one didn't look the least bit wilted. So I decided to save it for you by putting it in water."

"I would rather you'd left it where it was."

Her tone was terse. Joy cringed. "I'm sorry," she said.

"Let me grab my case notes. Do you mind if I put you on hold?"

"No, of course not."

The detective returned a minute later. "Okay, you told me you gave a report to Officer Williams. I've pulled that report and see that you've been seeing these roses first thing in the morning but randomly. It's always the exact same type of rose, and they appear to be fresh. Never another color or another type of flower. Never wilted or showing signs of having been left out more than just a few hours. Is that right? Not on certain days or at certain intervals?"

"Yes, that's right. All exactly the same, and I never know when one will appear."

"Okay. Tell me about the rose you found this morning. It fits with the pattern? Same flower, same condition?"

"Exactly." Joy paused. "I told Officer Williams that this rose isn't a common variety that just anyone could pick up at a garden center or florist."

"Go on," Detective Osborne said.

"It's special. Unique." Joy paused again. "I've never seen one like it, and I haven't been able to find a match to it in all the research

I've done. I was a member of the rose society in Houston before I moved here. I'm no expert, but I do have a decent working knowledge of roses and know how to identify them. This one has me baffled."

When the detective said nothing, Joy continued. "I've tried to propagate previous cuttings, but so far I've only gotten leaves. No blooms. I'm going to a garden club meeting tomorrow morning where the speaker is a woman known for her expertise in that topic."

Silence fell between Joy and the police officer. Then finally, Detective Osborne spoke.

"Here's the thing with the rose we took into evidence. It's withered and dying. It's sitting right here in front of me, and it's pitiful looking even though I'm trying to keep it alive."

"Put a baby aspirin in the water," Joy suggested. "That'll perk it up a little and extend the life of the bloom. An old florist's trick, but a good one."

"Oh, thanks. I'll try that." The detective sighed. "I wish you hadn't taken the rose off the statue's base. There may be something in the location of the flower that means something."

"I'm so sorry," Joy repeated. "I didn't think."

"It's okay. Next time you see one there—if there is a next time—please take a photograph first. Maybe call a security guard or the Charleston PD first."

"Yes, I will. I promise. If it means anything, in my experience the placing of the rose never varies, not that there's a lot of room on the statue's base." Joy sighed. "Well, I guess there is now."

"We're going to fix that soon," Detective Osborne said. "Most of us on the force have had a stay at Mercy Hospital or known someone who has. We appreciate what you guys do there. I hope we can catch the perpetrators," she said. "This is personal for us."

"Thank you for that," said Joy. "Without the Angel of Mercy standing outside the hospital, it feels like we've lost more than just a piece of art. Part of our history is missing." She paused. "Please don't take offense, but you appear to be an experienced detective."

"I've been around a while." Detective Osborne chuckled. "So yes, I am. And no offense taken."

"Okay, well, in your experience," Joy began, "what are the odds that we'll get the statue back?"

Silence stretched for a moment. "I wish I knew," the detective said on an exhale of breath.

Joy stayed busy for the next few hours with customers and deliveries. When she finally got a break, she decided to call Evelyn over in the records department. Her friend answered on the first ring.

"Good morning." Joy consulted the clock on the wall over the sink. "I guess I should say good afternoon. I didn't realize how late it was getting."

"You caught me at a good time. What's up?"

"I found another rose on the base of the statue this morning. I called Detective Osborne to let her know."

"I see," she said. "And Detective Osborne is the police officer who gave us her card on Wednesday, right?"

"Yes. That's the one. So, during our conversation I told her I had tried to propagate the roses I've found there in the past. It's not a variety I've ever seen or can find online."

"Interesting. Someone is making special flowers for the angel?"

"It appears so," Joy said. "But I've never had any luck getting one of the stems to bloom. They'll root just fine, but no flowers have appeared. I would love to do that so there would be living evidence of whatever type of Noisette this is." She paused. "That's where you come in."

"Me?" More laughter. "I love you dearly, Joy, but I know for a fact that you've set aside a special plot in your backyard for my cast-offs. Gardening is not my superpower, and making new roses grow from an old one is certainly beyond my abilities."

"Attending a meeting with me isn't though." Before Evelyn could protest, Joy hurried to continue. "There's an expert rosarian speaking at a garden club meeting. Her specialty is propagating roses. I've heard of her technique—she actually uses honey and some kind of bottle or jar—but the book where she describes it isn't for sale yet. It will, however, be available at the meeting."

Silence.

Then the sound of papers shuffling on Evelyn's end of the phone. Finally her friend sighed. "When is it?"

"Tomorrow morning." She hesitated, knowing that Evelyn was a night owl on the weekends. "At ten o'clock."

Evelyn groaned. "And I need to be there with you because why?"

"Because I don't want to go alone. I know this sounds like I'm talking about a junior high party, but it's just awkward to be the new person at a meeting. And my neighbor will be there. She's been inviting me for months."

"See," Evelyn said brightly. "You will know someone there."

"My neighbor is Claudia Guest."

"Oh."

Because Garrison rarely had time to take calls that weren't scheduled in advance, Claudia had taken to calling Evelyn instead of wasting time leaving messages for the administrator. Each time, the subject had something to do with the Angel of Mercy statue and Claudia's determination to provide a better home for it than the spot where it rested outside the hospital.

Or rather the spot where it used to rest.

"I've been dodging her calls since the angel went missing," Evelyn said. "She thought she had an ally in me because I'm the keeper of the records and a history buff. I think she expected me to agree with her that the statue belonged in the Charleston Museum. She even told me I ought to have a conversation with my husband about the history of Charleston so I would understand the Angel of Mercy's value to the community. Can you believe that?"

Evelyn's husband, James Perry, was the dean of the history department at the College of Charleston. If anyone knew about local history, it was him.

"Here's the rub, Joy. James told me that a colleague did his doctoral thesis on the origins of the statue, and the story of who paid for what and whose family gets the credit is not so clear. In fact, it isn't clear at all."

"Really?" Joy said. "I thought Claudia's family was responsible."

"They're one of two possibilities, according to James's colleague. Claudia traces her lineage through the Butler family line. That's her maiden name. But there's another family, the Fords, who factor into the story."

"How so?"

Evelyn chuckled. "It's what they call the 'pay or pose' question," she said. "Who paid for the statue and who was the poser who only claimed to? Though it's lost to history which was which. Ask a Butler and you'll get one answer, and if you could find a Ford, you'd get another."

"So the Fords no longer live in Charleston?"

"James's colleague couldn't find any to contribute to the thesis," Evelyn said. "Though I'm sure they're out there. It's up to someone with an interest to trace the tree that far back. But if you listen to Claudia, there's only one right answer and it's that Howard Butler paid for that statue, and the only way a Ford was involved was that one of them posed for it."

"I had no idea," Joy said. "Charleston history is fascinating."

"Certainly, it's rarely boring," Evelyn said. "In any case, the last thing I want to do is be cornered by Claudia Guest at a garden club meeting so she can tell me she was right about protecting the statue. Because she was, if you get down to it. Had we pushed to move the Angel of Mercy to the museum, we wouldn't be having this conversation right now, would we?"

"Actually, we might, because I really want to get my hands on that book, and I don't want to go alone," Joy said.

"I don't suppose you can just sneak in, buy a book, and leave, can you?" Evelyn asked. "I would drive the getaway car and buy you lunch after. You could name the place, and I'll pick up the tab."

Joy laughed. "No, it's not that easy. But I get your point. I'll call Anne and see if she wants to go. She's usually busy with something related to her granddaughter, but maybe she can spare a few hours in the morning." She paused. "I may be buying her lunch to get her to say yes."

"Now you're talking," Evelyn said with a laugh. "If you do, call me, and I'll meet the two of you there. Better yet—because I figure Anne will be nice and go with you unless she absolutely can't—why don't we get together for a late lunch after the meeting? You can tell me all about propagating nosegays."

"Noisettes," Joy corrected. "And yes, that sounds like a good idea. Let's plan on it. I'll call Anne then text you with the details."

Joy said her goodbyes to Evelyn then reached for her cell phone to call Anne. Friday was not her day to volunteer, so she would either be at home or at the church.

"I heard you got an assistant," Anne said when she picked up the phone. "That's not quite an intern, but it seems like God is working, doesn't it?"

"Well, hello to you too," Joy said. "It sure does. I'm still not sure how He pulled it off, but He certainly did."

"Really? That is interesting. So what's going on up there today?"

Joy caught her friend up on the details of finding the Noisette and making a report to the detective. Then she mentioned Claudia's garden club meeting and her purpose for wanting to go tomorrow. "The thing is," she said, "the rose is fresh as of this morning, and who knows if there will be another opportunity to propagate another one? Whoever's leaving them may decide not to leave anymore. I want to go to the meeting, but I need a favor."

"Anything," Anne said. "Can I call you back later this afternoon? Addie is leaving in an hour for a sleepover, and I won't see her again until tomorrow evening. How is my granddaughter old enough for sleepovers already? They grow so fast. But she'll have so much fun. The girls are going to the South Carolina Aquarium tomorrow."

"I've heard about that," Joy said, "but I haven't been there yet. Isn't that the one with the three-story shark tank?"

"It is," said Anne. "Last time we were there I think there were at least ten sharks in it, and all kinds of other animals and fish. It's one of Charleston's claims to fame—it's the deepest tank in the country. But my favorites are always the river otters. I could watch them for hours chasing each other and zipping down water slides."

Joy smiled. "I hope Addie has a great time. Why don't you call me this evening? I'll be home. I can tell you this much now. Here's the favor: in exchange for going with me to a garden club meeting at ten tomorrow morning, I'm buying lunch, and Evelyn is joining us."

"For the meeting?" Anne asked.

"For lunch," Joy said.

"I see." There was a pause. "Well, all right. I'll call you later and we can talk about it."

"Thank you, Anne. I feel awful for Garrison and want to do everything I can to help provide the police the information they need to find the Angel of Mercy."

"What does Garrison have to do with the theft?"

"I'll tell you when you've got time to talk."

They said their goodbyes and hung up. Joy tucked the phone into her pocket and lifted her eyes heavenward. "Thank You, Lord, for friends."

The gift shop door opened, and Angela bounded in. Then she stepped back to hold the door open for a fair-haired woman about Angela's age.

Before Joy could greet her, Angela asked the woman, "You're here for flowers, aren't you?"

It wasn't the first time since Angela began working that Joy had seen her make a guess as to what the customer wanted before he or she made a request. Thus, when the woman nodded, Joy was not surprised.

Angela led her over to the display of flowers and pointed out a spray of white roses arranged amid sprigs of eucalyptus. The woman's eyes widened. "White roses are her favorite. How did you know?"

Angela shrugged. "I just know sometimes. Would you like a pink ribbon, or is your friend not into traditional gender colors?"

Again the woman appeared flabbergasted. "Pink, please. And again, how did you know she was here to have her baby girl?"

"I just know sometimes," Angela said again with a shrug. "Will you be taking this to her, or would you like us to deliver them?"

The customer looked past her to make eye contact with Joy. Then she returned her attention to Angela. "Deliver them, please. She's my boyfriend's sister, so I don't want to be a pest and go back up after I've already said goodbye."

"Do you want to pick out a card while I put a bow on these? That section of small cards is free with the purchase of flowers."

Angela left the woman to peruse the card selection and walked over to where Joy was standing. "How do you do that?" Joy asked her.

She pressed past Joy to move toward the station where the ribbons were kept. "It just comes to me."

When the customer arrived at the counter with a card, Joy handed her a pen from the cup beside the cash register and watched while she wrote out a name. "You'll be able to find her room number, right? I should have written it down when I went up to see her."

Joy looked at the card. MAKENZIE SMITH. "I'm sure we can find the room. There can't be more than one Makenzie Smith here with a newborn daughter."

The woman produced a credit card, which Joy used to pay for the transaction. As she handed the card back, the customer placed a business card on the table.

LETICIA BROWN, VICE PRESIDENT AND GENERAL MANAGER, BROWN CONSTRUCTION, INC.

Joy looked up at her. "Do you happen to be related to an India Ainsworth-Brown? I'm looking forward to hearing her speak at the garden club tomorrow."

Leticia's smile went south. "Yes, she's my mother," was her terse reply.

Seeking to close whatever wound she had inadvertently opened, Joy hurried to add, "Brown Construction built my new garage and is doing my remodel. Richard Bowe is my architect. He recommended your company highly, and I'm so happy he did."

"I'm glad to hear it," she said, perking up. "You're in good hands with Richard. And us, of course."

Joy smiled. "Yes, absolutely."

Angela fluffed the pink lacy bow as she moved toward them. "Do you think she'll like this? If you think it's too girly, I can replace it with a plain pink ribbon."

"It's perfect," Leticia pronounced then said goodbye and left.

Joy slid the business card into the drawer beneath the counter and returned her attention to Angela as her phone rang. She glanced at the screen to see who was calling then slipped into the back room to answer.

"I just have a minute," Shirley said. "That nurse I told you about who was missing for an hour? A picture of her just showed up on her Facebook account with a caption that says, 'Sneaking out to see the angel.'" She paused. "Joy, the statue is in the picture, but it's not in its place."

"Where is it?" Joy asked. "Can you tell?"

"I can't, but it's definitely not the hospital," Shirley said. "I called that detective to tell her. The nurse's page is private, so I sent her a screenshot in case the post disappears."

"Who's the nurse?"

"Nancy Jones. Do you know her?"

She chose her words carefully. There was no need to bring Evelyn into this until she had a chance to speak to her privately. "No, but I know who does."

Chapter Seven

Joy waited until she knew Evelyn would be home from work and then called her. When the call went to voice mail, she hung up without leaving a message.

A few hours later, just as Joy was preparing for bed, her phone rang. Joy's heart lurched. Rarely did her phone ring this late. She looked at the screen. It was Evelyn. Though Evelyn was a night owl, she knew Joy was not.

"I'm so sorry to call at this hour, Joy," Evelyn said breathlessly, "but I've got to tell you what happened tonight. You're not going to believe it."

Joy settled back against the pillows. "Okay," she said. "What happened?"

"Remember that place you told me about where you get those scented candles you like?"

"Curiosities & Candles Emporium?"

"Yes, that's the one." Evelyn paused. "James was attending a lecture tonight, so I thought I'd go over there and look for a few little things for Nancy's shower."

Joy thought of interrupting her and telling her Shirley's news about Nancy, but she kept silent and allowed Evelyn to continue. There would be time to tell her Shirley's story when this tale was told.

"I didn't think to check the hours, so when I got there I was surprised to find the door locked and the lights off in the store, though I could see there was a light on in the storeroom or whatever is in the back. I guess they close early on weekdays."

"I think Flavia closes at five. She's the owner. Richard Bowe's sister, actually."

"Your architect? I didn't know that. Well, anyway, I went back to my car and sat there a minute checking messages and seeing if I could find the grocery list I thought I'd put into my phone. I truly have a love-hate relationship with this new gadget James insisted on buying me. I miss the days when a flip phone would do the job."

"Then what happened?" Joy urged, anxious to get her turn to talk.

"Well, I decided to give up on all of it and go home. Only I got a phone call from my aunt Peach who lives over in Brunswick. By the time I managed to get off the phone with her, it had to be half past eight at least. I pulled out and turned right at the corner to head home. And that's when I saw them."

"Saw who?"

"I don't know. The alley behind the building was all in shadow, so I couldn't see faces. They were behind the candle shop," Evelyn said. "There was a dark-colored van—sort of a small moving van— parked there. Two people in coveralls were carrying something to the van. One was bigger than the other, but my guess is both were men."

"What were they carrying?"

"That's where this gets really strange," she said. "Joy, it looked like they were carrying a mummy wrapped in white cloth. Then it occurred to me. They might have the Angel of Mercy under that cloth. It was certainly the right size or at least looked to be from where I was sitting."

"Did you call the police?"

"I did. While I was on the phone with the desk sergeant, the men in the jumpsuits got into the van and sat there a minute. I couldn't see a license plate, because it was dark. Then the headlights came on, and there was too much glare to see anything."

"Surely you got the plate number when they drove out. I know that alley, and there's only two ways that van could have exited."

"You're right about that," Evelyn said. "I don't know if they saw me and decided not to head toward me or what, but they backed all the way to the other street and took off in a flash. I never saw anything go backward so fast in my life. Well, not since my cousin Izzy got cold feet at her wedding and ran off just before the preacher started the vows. Anyway, the sergeant said he would see that Detective Osborne got the report tomorrow."

"That's it? You'd think they might have sent a car out to look for the van," Joy said.

"I couldn't give them much to go on. Just that the van was dark and that two men in jumpsuits were in the cab."

Joy let out a long breath. "And I thought I was the one with the urgent news about the statue. It looks like your sighting beats my social media photo."

"What's this?" Evelyn asked.

Joy gave her the details. "So, what do you know about Nancy Jones? I'm about to text you a picture that Anne sent earlier. It looks like our wedding shower honoree just might have a dark side to her."

"Nancy? Impossible. She's as sweet as she can be." Evelyn paused. "Email it, please. I'm having a time with this phone, remember?"

Joy put the phone on speaker and sent the email. A moment later Evelyn gasped. "That's her. But what in the world is she doing?"

"She's standing in front of the statue," Joy said.

"But where is the statue?" Evelyn demanded.

"That, my friend, is the sixty-four-thousand-dollar question."

"Good morning, ladies and gentlemen," Claudia Guest said. "I am thrilled that we have a nice turnout today at our little Petals and Plants group for the last day of National Gardening Week."

Their host wore an ivory sheath dress and matching ivory sandals with a sapphire-blue scarf. Even from where she sat with Anne, Joy could see matching sapphire earrings sparkling from beneath Claudia's chin-length blond bob.

Anne leaned toward Joy. "Petals and Plants? I thought it was just the Charleston Garden Club."

"No, the Garden Club of Charleston is one of the oldest garden clubs in America," Joy told her. "They do the House and Garden Tours and things like that. From what I've read in the neighborhood newsletter, this group is Claudia's pet project and is significantly smaller, as you can see. She started it about ten years ago when she lost her bid to become president of the bigger group."

"She admits that?" Anne asked.

"Oh yes," Joy said. "It's in her bio in every newsletter. Right up there with a mention of her doctoral thesis on Charleston Noisette roses."

Anne raised her eyebrows. "Well, at least she's consistent. And very well dressed for a club where you dig in the dirt."

"I'm pretty sure this garden club doesn't actually do any digging at their meetings," Joy assured her. "It's more of a discussion of gardening. And I really appreciate you coming and hopefully deflecting any conversation about the statue. I don't want to hear about how Evelyn should have listened to Claudia about putting it in a museum."

Anne patted her hand. "It's what friends do. Besides, you're paying for lunch."

"True." Joy lowered her voice. "I'm also hoping I can find out who in the community is cultivating a Noisette rose that looks like the one on the statue."

"How do we find that out?" Anne asked.

"I'm not sure." Joy looked around and counted about three dozen gardeners assembled in the small room at the main branch of the Charleston County Public Library. Two tables were positioned at the front of the room on either side of a carved wooden lectern that looked to be as old as the building itself.

The table on the right was covered in a green cloth and filled with seedlings in small black pots. To the left of the lectern, the table wore a matching green cloth but held a stack of what must be the book Joy had come to purchase. So far there was no sign of India Ainsworth-Brown.

Claudia's gaze landed on Joy. In hopes of evading detection, she and Anne had waited outside in the library until just before the meeting would be called to order. Then they slipped in and chose a row in the back of the room behind a trio of blond ladies whose hair had been teased halfway to heaven.

"Welcome, everyone," Claudia continued, her attention sweeping around the room as her smile rose. "And a special welcome to our first-time visitors and honored guests."

As if on cue, the door swung open and India Ainsworth-Brown swept inside followed close behind by Leticia. Unlike yesterday, India's daughter wore no hint of a smile.

India had exercised a flair for the dramatic by arriving in an all-black sheath dress, gloves, and matching cape and hat despite the June heat. Leticia carried a stack of books and a leather portfolio. She was dressed for a day at the office with navy trousers and a tailored white shirt, her light brown hair pulled back into a low ponytail.

"India, darling," Claudia called. "Everyone, this is our guest of honor, India Ainsworth-Brown. Please give her a warm welcome."

As the applause began, India reached Claudia and whispered something to her. Claudia nodded then reached for the microphone again.

"And this is her daughter, Leticia."

"Daughter?" Anne whispered. "Looks more like her secretary."

"I met her at the hospital yesterday," Joy whispered. "She seemed nice."

Claudia led the ladies to chairs that had been set up behind the book table. Leticia added the books she was carrying to the stack already there but held the portfolio in her lap. India remained standing long enough to give a quick hug to Claudia and then a wave to the crowd.

"We are quite excited to have you here, India," Claudia continued. "As a rosarian myself, I was thrilled to get a sneak peek at your new book." She turned to address the crowd. "As many of you know, my doctoral thesis on the Noisette roses of Charleston has become a classic, so I was quite surprised when I read India's method of propagating these lovely blooms. I don't want to give too much away, but I can tell you that it involves honey and a process that did cause me to raise my eyebrows a bit."

Joy's attention shifted to India, who appeared to be having a hard time not scowling. Her daughter, however, was looking out the window and seemed oblivious to anything happening in the meeting.

Claudia shifted the topic to business matters and finally back to their speaker. "Enough about the annual plant sale," she declared. "Just come up afterward and pick up your seedlings, but don't forget to put your money in the basket. The more you donate, the more this organization can do for the city of Charleston."

"The more posters with her face on it can be printed," one of the women in front of Joy whispered to her companion, who nodded.

"And now we come to the part of the meeting many of you have been waiting for. Perhaps she is the reason you're attending." Claudia once again found Joy in the crowd, and this time she smiled. "Though we would like to have you here every month, we're glad you've finally chosen to spend your Saturday morning with us."

A smattering of applause filled the silence that followed her comments. Then Claudia nodded.

"India needs no introduction. She is a Charleston treasure, and I will leave it at that. Ladies and gentlemen, my friend, master gardener and rosarian extraordinaire, India Ainsworth-Brown."

Claudia took a seat on the left side of the podium behind the seedling table. Though her attention was now on India, Joy could still feel her neighbor's gaze.

"It was like she was talking to you," Anne whispered. "What's up with that?"

"She's been inviting me here for a while now," Joy said. "So maybe she was."

The guest of honor arrived at the podium with a broad smile. "I'm so very glad to be here this morning," India said, her voice holding the regulated tones of a well-to-do Southern woman. "I know some of you have your doubts about my method for propagating roses, but I hope to make believers of you all before I'm done."

India slid a quick glance toward Claudia and then continued. "And yes, it does involve honey. Worse," she said as she put on a horrified expression and clasped at her neck with her bejeweled hands, "you can use old plastic water bottles to achieve my results."

The audience laughed. Claudia did not.

India proceeded to walk the group through the steps to propagate roses using these unusual items. A slide show, operated by Leticia, offered proof of her results. After a few more minutes spent talking up her newest book, India opened the floor to questions.

Seizing the opportunity, Joy raised her hand. Eventually, India called on her.

"This is related to propagation," Joy said after she'd stood up. "From what I've seen of the preview of your book online, you have a chapter about creating new varieties of roses."

"I do, yes," India said. "It's a favorite topic of mine. I would write an entire book about it if my publisher would let me. How can I help you?"

"My question is specific to Noisettes." Joy paused. "Is it possible to propagate a Noisette rose that would be the customary cream color in the outer petals but have a crimson color in its center? And if so, do you know anyone who has managed that?"

Before India could answer, Claudia stood. "Absolutely impossible. Noisettes are by their very nature a pale rose. The first Noisette was raised as a hybrid seedling by our own John Champneys. The flower was grafted from a China Rose called Parson's Pink and the Rosa Moschata, also known as the musk rose. Grafting can add a measure of color—and has, as seen in the many varieties of colorful Noisettes available now—but crimson? No. Deep pink such as the Meteor is as close as we've come. And a red center in the middle of a cream Noisette?" She shook her head. "It cannot be done."

But it has was on the tip of Joy's tongue.

"Not so fast, Claudia," India said. "Are you sure about that?"

Chapter Eight

A TENSE MOMENT PASSED BETWEEN the two women. Neither appeared willing to look away.

"Show me an example then," Claudia said evenly through clenched jaws. Her eyes cut to Joy. "One that hasn't been obviously faked."

India laughed. "Now that is impossible. I don't have one. But as far as we've come in adding color to our Noisettes and creating so many varieties of other types of roses? I just can't imagine that we're unable to achieve something like that." She offered Joy a smile. "Does that answer your question?"

"It does," Joy said, deciding not to enter the fray with what she knew. "Thank you. Now if I could, I have just one more question."

"Of course," India said sweetly. "Perhaps Claudia and I will agree on this one, unlike our opinions on the pay-or-pose question."

What India appeared to mean as a joke seemed to be anything but humorous to Claudia. Instead, the group's host appeared poised to snatch the microphone away from India and order them all to go home.

Joy instantly recognized the words Evelyn had used to refer to the origins of the Angel of Mercy. That India was prodding

Claudia in such a public way seemed odd at best and mean-spirited at worst.

Slowly Claudia lowered herself onto her chair once more, but her cordial expression did not return. Joy sighed. These two definitely had a history that went well beyond roses.

Joy put on a smile. "All right, well, it's about propagating a rose from a cutting that has been in water."

"A safer subject," India quipped. "Go on."

"Let's say I have a rose that I've had in water for a few days. The bloom is fading, but I want to see if I can root the stem and grow another plant like it. So, I need to graft the stem from the fading flower to grow an identical bloom, right?"

"That's right," India said. "The stem dictates the flower. And as long as the stem is still healthy when you attempt to root it, it shouldn't matter that it's been in water for a few days. Though I will caution you that I wouldn't go much longer than three or four days in water."

"So what if the stem is from a hybrid? Let's say I've crossed two Noisettes and created a unique bud. A cutting of the original stem would yield whichever variety I had in the stem, but if I took a cutting of one of the branches, I should get a rooting of the hybrid flower, right?"

India seemed to consider the question for a moment. Then she nodded. "Yes, that's right."

Joy thought of the other Noisette roses she'd kept in the past and the few that she'd managed to root but not see blooming. "So the final part of my question is, how difficult is it to root a hybrid from its own branch and get a bloom?"

"The general answer is it's no more difficult than rooting any other branch. However, it has been my experience that the further away from the original flower the hybrid gets, the more difficult it is to replicate it." She paused. "In essence, my opinion is we can make a number of crazy-looking flowers, be they roses or any other type of bloom, but making them once and then repeating that happy accident again and again? That's another story."

"Thank you. That answers my question." Joy sat down and glanced over at Anne, who smiled.

After a few more questions were answered, Claudia stood to thank India and adjourn the meeting. When Claudia stepped away from the podium, a volunteer in a green apron with the Petals and Plants logo on the pocket hurried to the seedling table to help those who wished to buy plants.

"Don't forget to buy India's book. And if anyone does try her method, I want a report—including pictures—next month. You know what we say here. If we can't see it, then it didn't happen." Claudia reached to turn off the microphone.

"My book has lots of pictures of my successes," India said sweetly just before the sound turned off.

Joy joined the line of attendees waiting for the opportunity to buy a copy of India's book. When she reached the front of the line, Leticia handed her a copy.

"Thank you, Leticia," she told the young woman as she handed her a credit card. "It's very nice of you to be here with your mother today."

"It's what I do lately," she said, returning the credit card and receipt once the transaction was complete. "When I'm not doing everything else down at—"

"Hello there," India interrupted, reaching for the book. "To whom may I autograph this book?"

"Joy." She handed the book to India. "I found your presentation very interesting."

India completed her signature then closed the book and returned it to Joy. "And I found your questions even more interesting. This rose you speak of, is it real, or theoretical?"

"It's nothing I've been able to replicate," Joy said. The truth and yet probably not the answer India expected.

India seemed poised to say more. Then Leticia nudged her.

"Yes, well, I hope you enjoy the book."

Joy tucked the book into her bag and moved on to allow the next person her turn with the author. She made her way to where Anne was waiting for her near the door.

They got all the way out into the corridor before Claudia Guest caught up with them. "I cannot believe you were going to leave without saying goodbye."

"Oh, I'm sorry," Joy said. "You were busy, and I didn't want to interrupt you." She nodded toward Anne. "This is my friend Anne Mabry."

"Pleased to meet you, Anne." Claudia turned to Joy. "Might I have a word with you in private?"

Joy and Anne exchanged glances.

"I'll just be a minute," Claudia reassured them.

"I'll go see if the library book I ordered has come in." Anne smiled at Claudia. "It was nice meeting you."

"Likewise." Claudia hardly waited a moment before beginning. "You can tell Evelyn for me that I take no satisfaction in saying I told you so, but ..." She paused and shook her head. "No, I won't say it. The loss of the Angel of Mercy is too awful to discuss right now."

"It is terrible, but I've been assured by the administrator and the police that all leads are being followed. They hope to return it soon."

"Hope will not get that statue returned," Claudia snapped. "And even if it does, then what? We've just seen how easy she is to steal. How long before someone else has a go at it?"

"I'm not sure what you want me to say, Claudia. I hate that it's missing, but a lot of people feel that way."

"A lot of people are not descended from the very hands that sculpted that statue. Or the person who paid for it."

"About that," Joy said. "I wonder if you've got some kind of papers showing that to be true. I would love to read them. The history of Charleston is fascinating."

Color climbed into Claudia's cheeks, and her expression went blank. "Papers? As in what? A sales receipt?" Her clear tone conveyed her contempt for the question. "I understand you're new to the city, but you do understand that 150 years ago one did not simply write up a sales invoice or tuck a credit card receipt into his wallet after commissioning such a masterpiece."

"No, of course not, but there must be some sort of record," Joy insisted.

"There is," Claudia said, "a record passed down through the generations as fact. From my grandfather from his and so on back to the original Butler who commissioned the angel."

"Do you have any idea who sculpted the piece? And who the angel's model was?"

"Also lost to time, I'm afraid," Claudia said. "The family has done their searches, but there's just no record."

"The Butler family?"

Claudia nodded.

"What about the Fords?"

"Who told you about the Fords?" she said evenly.

She thought of the doctoral thesis that Evelyn had told her about. "I heard about it from someone who researched the origins of the statue."

"Don't believe everything you hear, Joy."

Before Joy could respond, Claudia continued, "As I was saying, the statue's loss is absolutely magnified by the fact that someone is continuing to place Noisettes at the base. And yes, I know it's happening, though I've yet to see one. I read the police report."

Joy remained silent. If Claudia knew about the Noisettes left at the statue, would she know from the questions Joy asked India that Joy had one in her possession?

"I have tried to speak to Garrison Baker," Claudia continued. "I've also tried to reach the records department supervisor. No one is taking my calls. So I want you to deliver a message. I will be marshaling the board into action. If Garrison Baker is so careless as to allow the statue to be stolen on his watch, then he needs to be dismissed."

"That's quite harsh, Claudia. I don't see how the fault for the theft of the Angel of Mercy can belong to anyone except the person or persons who took it."

Claudia shook her head, her eyes tired. "And that is where we'll have to agree to disagree. Just pass my promise along, please. And it is a promise. The Guests have considerable pull at the hospital, and

I have it on good authority that there's a budget approval meeting coming up soon. If Mr. Baker won't take my call, then maybe he'll listen to you and call me."

"I can't promise to pass on a message like that," Joy said.

Claudia's eyes narrowed. "Can't, or won't?"

"Won't," Joy said.

"Because you're upset that I don't believe a two-toned Noisette like the one you described exists?"

Joy shook her head. "I didn't create that bloom, but if you've read the police report then you know it's real. I wonder if anyone here might have created it. If Charleston is like Houston, the rosarian community is a small one." She paused, modulating her voice so that her tone was gentle. "I miss the statue very much and would love to discover who has taken it. I have to wonder if the Noisettes are connected to the theft."

Claudia threw up her hands. "Look, if I can't get anyone to take my call, then how do you propose I let them know what I think?" Her eyes blazed, her purpose seemingly renewed. "Because what I think matters."

Joy didn't miss a beat. "Of course it does. There's a suggestion box in the lobby." She glanced down at her watch and smiled. "I'm sorry, but I've got a lunch I can't miss. Take care, Claudia. And please know you're always welcome in the gift shop for coffee."

"Even if I'm not welcome in the hospital?"

"Always," Joy said with another smile. "And I mean that."

Claudia nodded. "I know you do. And forgive me for my zeal. I'm just so passionate about my family history and the things related to it."

"There's nothing to forgive," Joy told her. "And for your sake, I hope you're right about the Butlers and Fords. I can't imagine it would be pleasant to find out you were wrong about that."

"But I'm not, Joy."

Joy and Claudia said their goodbyes and then Joy joined Anne at the circulation counter. "You survived," Anne joked. "Everything okay?"

"Everything is fine. Claudia's having trouble getting her opinion heard. She's upset, which is understandable."

"I'm surprised, given her connections with the hospital," Anne said as they stepped out into the June heat.

"Oh yes," Joy said. "Depending on who you listen to, her ancestors—the Butlers—are responsible for the statue being where it is—or rather where it was."

"No wonder she's protective of the angel."

"And devastated that she's gone," Joy said. "She's blaming Garrison Baker. I'm worried about what she will do."

"What do you think she'll do?"

"She's threatened to go to the board and get rid of Garrison."

"We can't let that happen," Anne said.

"No," Joy agreed. "We can't."

After a short walk, Joy and Anne arrived at Henrietta's, a lovely bistro in the lobby of the Dewberry Hotel on Meeting Street. They crossed the black-and-white tiled floor and joined Evelyn at a table by the window.

A waiter came to take their drink orders, and then Joy and Anne filled Evelyn in on the events at the meeting. By the time they'd placed their lunch orders, Evelyn was bursting with news.

"I got a call from Detective Osborne. There's no news on the owners of the van—not that I expected there would be—but I'm going to be served with a subpoena for Alan Parker's hospital records on Monday morning. She wanted to give me a heads-up that it was coming."

"That was nice of her," Joy said. "It didn't take long for her to figure out who we were talking about. She's a smart lady. And speaking of ladies, I'm going to make sure to speak with Flavia Bowe today. I want to know whether she knows about something going on behind her building last night. And if she was part of it."

"She should know," Evelyn said.

"I agree." Anne nodded. "If I were dependent on a store for my livelihood I would be sure I knew what was happening there all the time."

"Maybe she's not," Joy said.

"Not what?" Anne asked.

"Not dependent on the store. I mean, she seems so nice and the least likely person who would traffic in stolen goods. She's Richard Bowe's sister, for goodness' sake, and they're from an old Charleston family." Joy shook her head. "And yet I am only basing that assumption on my conversations with her. She could be perfectly nice but up to her eyeballs in trouble and be able to hide it well."

"Honestly, do you think that's the case?" Evelyn asked.

"I don't have a clue, but I'm going to talk to her. In the meantime, there's another reason I wanted us to meet today."

"This sounds ominous." Evelyn reached to take a sip of her iced tea.

"I know we're all worried about what's happened to the Angel of Mercy, but from what I've heard, there's much more at stake now than just the return of a statue."

"Like what?" Anne asked.

"I'll start at the beginning. I talked to Garrison Baker, and what he told me really caused me some serious concern." She paused. "For him and for the hospital. The reason those cameras didn't function right on the night the statue was taken is because having them repaired wasn't in the budget. Nor were the funds to pay for security guards to patrol outside." Joy took a breath. "All of that traces back to the hospital administrator not spending the money on those things."

"But that's not fair," Anne said. "He can't be blamed if the board wouldn't give him the money to spend. Right?"

"I agree, but he is being blamed," Joy said. "Not publicly that I've heard of, but I just had a conversation with Claudia Guest where she flat out told me she's going to the board to see what can be done about him."

"You mean she wants him fired?" Evelyn asked. "Because the Angel of Mercy was taken on his watch?"

"Exactly." Joy gave it a moment's consideration. "Though what she really wants is the statue to be returned."

"And put into a museum," Anne added. "Something that's sadly more likely now. If it can be found at all."

"I would very much like to see it found," Joy said.

"As would I," Evelyn said while Anne nodded in agreement.

"Okay," Joy said, "we need a plan. I wish we could include Shirley in our efforts, but her schedule is so wacky now, I think we don't need to add anything to her plate."

"Right," Evelyn said. "Why don't I have a talk with Nancy? I've looked at that picture more times than I can count, but I cannot for the life of me figure out where it was taken. The background is blurred, but it's definitely not the hospital building."

"I agree," Anne said. "I showed it to Ralph, and he said it looked like the background was digitally altered in some way."

"What do you mean?" Joy asked.

"He said it was impossible to tell from Nancy's picture, but either the person taking the photo didn't want the background to be identifiable or they were able to superimpose the image of Nancy and the Angel of Mercy over another image of a background to make it look as if the two were one real photograph. Photoshopping, basically."

"Why would an on-duty nurse disappear for an hour in the middle of the night then post a photo of herself with the angel statue?" Joy glanced from Anne to Evelyn. Both shrugged. "I guess we add this to the list of questions. Now just one more. Who is her fiancé, Evelyn? Have you met him?"

"I haven't," Evelyn said. "But she showed me a picture of him, and he's a handsome fellow. I think she said he's a banker or maybe a financial planner. Something like that."

"So not an IT guy or someone who might digitally alter pictures?" Joy asked.

Evelyn chuckled. "Nowadays any kid in junior high, or even younger, can digitally alter a picture. It's incredibly easy to do that kind of thing. For someone like me who works in a records department where determining the validity of a document is a big deal, this fact is supremely distressing."

"She's right," Anne agreed. "Still, she was absent from her job for an hour in the middle of the night. I don't volunteer on the night shift and I never have, but I can vouch for what Shirley said about staff members hiding away to take a much-needed nap. I can also vouch for Evelyn in that I've seen more than one visitor do something crazy."

"Like skateboarding down the halls in a hoodie," Evelyn said. "And outside, if that's the same one Norm was chasing when he hurt himself."

"Exactly." Joy sighed. "So to recap, I got nowhere with my line of questions about cultivating Noisette roses, Evelyn saw two people removing something that could be the statue from the back of Flavia's store—"

"Or one of the others that are on that row," Evelyn interjected. "When I talked to Detective Osborne today, she reminded me that there's a whole row of businesses that have their back entrances in that alley. I didn't actually see which door they came out of. I just saw them carrying the mummy to the van."

"Yes, right," Joy continued. "And other than the police looking into Alan Parker as a possible suspect, there are no other leads that we know about. There has to be more to it that than this. What is it we're not seeing?"

"Okay, this is crazy," Anne said tentatively. "But I was with you at the meeting."

"And thank you for that," Evelyn said with a grin.

Anne chuckled. "As I was saying, since no one was paying much attention to me, I was able to do a lot of watching while you were asking your questions, Joy." She paused, her expression now sober. "And I have to wonder if we're missing out on a possible suspect."

"Who?" Joy asked.

"Claudia Guest."

"Why in the world would Claudia Guest want to take the statue?" Evelyn demanded. "She's the one who's been so vocal about ..." She paused. "Of course. If the statue was taken, then it proves her point. Just like we've been saying. She had motive and opportunity."

Joy dug into her purse for a pen and something to write on. She came up with last week's grocery list. Turning it over, she wrote the word *Suspects* at the top of the page. Then, for point number one, she listed Claudia.

Then came Nancy followed by Alan Parker. "Who else had motive or opportunity?" Joy asked. "Or just flat out belongs on the list?"

"Flavia Bowe," Evelyn said. "After what I saw last night, she has to be on the list until we prove she doesn't."

Joy nodded. "All right. Well ... if there are no more names to go on for now, how about we finish our lunch, and then I'll pay a visit to Candles & Curiosities Emporium to speak with Flavia?"

After saying goodbye to the ladies, Joy set off in the direction of the store. She had been introduced to Curiosities & Candles Emporium on East Bay Street, which specialized in architectural salvage and their one-of-a-kind line of candles, not too long after arriving in Charleston.

Once in view of the historic brick building, she noticed that a poster for the Petals and Plants garden club meeting was still hanging in the window nearest the beautiful antique front door.

Joy smiled and reached for the ornate doorknob. Burnished copper bells jangled softly as she opened the door and stepped inside.

The lovely store, formerly the family home of owner Flavia Bowe, was filled to the rafters with an amazing mix of antiques, local treasures, and scented candles. Joy had met Flavia and her brother Richard when their mother was undergoing cancer treatment at Mercy Hospital a few months ago, and found them both to be lovely and creative souls.

Flavia still paid Joy the occasional visit to personally deliver the store's own brand of artisan candles that the gift shop sold. The gift shop couldn't keep the heavenly scented candles in stock. If the patients weren't buying them, the staff was snatching them up.

Still, Joy loved the chance to shop the aisles of the lovely store on East Bay.

No one was behind the counter, so she decided to step over to the candle aisle to pick up two of their Sage and Cotton candles for herself. On her way back to the center aisle, Joy spied a lovely set of wind chimes made from odd pieces of metal, spoons, and other salvaged material that would be perfect for Sabrina's patio.

Joy could have spent much more time browsing the merchandise, but she was here on a mission. She hurried to the counter to pay for her items.

When she reached the counter, Flavia stood with her back to Joy behind the antique gold cash register. To the right of the register, which had been modernized to accommodate the needs of a twenty-first century store, was a beautiful yellow cake stand that held a neatly stacked pyramid of the store's newest candle scent: Green Tomato Surprise.

A stack of flyers advertising the upcoming performance of *Night at the Museum* at the Charleston Museum on Meeting Street had been placed just to the side of the cake plate. Since Flavia's other passion was photography, it was likely she had taken the dramatic picture of her brother in historical garb that graced the flyer.

Looking more like a nineteenth-century sea captain than a twenty-first-century architect, the flame-haired Richard Bowe did reenactments in addition to the monthly *Night at the Museum* performances where he wore the costume of a landed gentry and enacted one-man shows from the time period. He was also known for his award-winning work restoring historic homes. Even though Joy's house wasn't historic, he'd done a marvelous job with her remodel.

The polar opposite of her big brother with the bigger personality, Flavia was tiny and soft-spoken with lovely strawberry blond hair that was almost always caught up in a long ponytail or a stylish messy bun when she was working in the shop. Today she wore a black button-down shirt over a black pencil skirt beneath her usual striped blue-and-white denim chef's apron with *C&C* monogrammed in gold script on the front. A pen with the same logo was stuck into her messy bun.

A chunky gold hoop necklace with a gold-dipped sand dollar sparkled at her neck, and a stack of gold bracelets clattered as she moved her free hand, gesturing as she spoke in whispered tones into her cell phone. Then her back stiffened, and her voice rose.

"Absolutely not! I will not be party to such a thing. If anyone even got a whiff of the fact that you were involved in such—" Flavia shook her head and rested her free hand on her hip, the gold bracelets sliding to her wrist.

"I don't care about the consequences. I can't keep bailing you out like this. I love you, but the answer is no."

Chapter Nine

Joy watched as Flavia moved to stand behind the vintage blue-and-white toile curtain that separated the stockroom from the front of the store. She was now mostly out of sight—other than a gap between the curtains that showed her back—but definitely not out of hearing range.

Thus, Joy could still see—and hear—Flavia continuing to argue with someone. Her concern grew.

The door jangled again, and two laughing young women with sun-streaked, honey-colored hair stepped inside. One wore a sundress in shades of coral and matching sandals while the other wore a pale yellow T-shirt with a Design is Mine by Coni Devine logo tucked into a pair of white shorts. She had finished off the ensemble with a pair of neon-pink Converse sneakers.

Immediately the woman in coral began extolling the virtues of the seafaring paintings on the wall nearest the door while the other recorded her with her phone. When they spied Joy watching them, the woman in the yellow T-shirt shrugged.

"We've looked everywhere for just the right painting to go over the fireplace. I'm recording Ava so we can remember where we were in case she changes her mind and wants to go back for another look."

Ava offered a grin that showed her brilliant white teeth, even from a distance. "I love everything I see and want to find a place for it. Coni here, she thinks like a decorator and …" She held up her hands to mimic quotation marks then continued. "… edits."

"Which is why you pay me to do your decorating," Coni quipped. "If I let you, you'd be negotiating for a copy of that horrid statue in front of Mercy Hospital."

Joy's ears perked up.

The woman she now knew as Ava shrugged. "It's a beautiful statue. You know it would look absolutely gorgeous in the pavilion next to the beach."

Coni shook her head. "A couple of issues with that idea. First, the statue isn't for sale. And second, the salt air would wreck it."

"Would not," Ava protested. "It's made of rock, not metal. And you know as well as I do, Coni, everything is for sale if you offer the right price to the right people."

Joy stifled a curt response. The Angel of Mercy statue was definitely not for sale at any price, no matter what this woman thought. Or at least it shouldn't be, though it might very well be the subject of bidding right now.

She walked over to where the ladies were standing. "I'm sorry to intrude, but did I hear you say something about the Angel of Mercy statue?"

Coni's attention swung in her direction while Ava seemed fixated on a picture frame covered in what appeared to be shards of wood. "Not the real one, of course. Nobody knows where that one is, unfortunately."

"No, of course," Joy said.

"But Coni could definitely get you a copy of it if you wanted one," Ava said, sparing Joy a quick glance. "She knows where to find everything."

"Is that right?" Joy said.

Coni shrugged. "I've ordered stranger things for clients. So sure, if you're looking to have a copy of a statue made—any statue— then I could probably source that for you. Everyone has their price."

"Interesting. Do you have a business card?" Joy asked.

The decorator turned around and gestured to her back. There in the middle of the T-shirt were all the particulars on how to reach her, including phone, fax, and email as well as a list of social media accounts. Below the list was one of those odd squares to scan in order to go to a website.

"Just take a photo, and you'll have it," Coni told her. "Now if you'll excuse me, I've got to get Ava back on track. If I don't supervise her, she wanders, and when she wanders she buys things I have to find a place for. And that is not fun."

"Sure. Thank you." Joy tucked her phone back into her pocket and watched as Coni headed toward the second aisle on the left nearest the door. Then Joy returned to her place at the counter where she could still see Flavia standing on the other side of the curtain.

"Look, there are the Estelle cake plates I told you about. You're going to absolutely die when you see how gorgeous these are," Coni told Ava. "They're from a local designer, and they are absolutely stunning. You'll have a hard time picking which one you want. Of course, I plan to help with that decision."

"I'm talking about a statue for my gazebo, and you want me to look at a cake plate?" Ava's bright smile went south. "My granny had one of those. I can't imagine what would make these special."

"Just wait and see," her decorator friend promised as she grabbed hold of Ava's arm to disappear with her down an aisle and out of Joy's sight. "Remember I sent you that article from *Southern Living* magazine about the lady who recreated and modernized her grandmother's glassware and serving pieces in gorgeous colors?"

A squeal of what had to be happiness split the air. Apparently the Estelle cake plates delivered what Coni promised. The squeal they induced in Ava apparently also got Flavia's attention.

"Look, I have customers," Flavia said. "I promise you don't want any of them overhearing this call. This conversation is over. And do not threaten me again!"

She disconnected the call but remained very still, her shoulders slumped and the phone clutched in her hand. Whatever the call was about, it had obviously affected Flavia deeply.

Joy waited a moment, thinking that the store owner would turn around. Then she cleared her throat.

Flavia startled and whirled around. Crimson quickly colored her cheeks as she tucked the phone into the pocket of her apron. There was a smile on her face that did not quite meet her eyes as she hurried toward the cash register.

Something was terribly wrong.

"How nice to see you again, Joy," Flavia said in a voice that retained some of the tense tone from her phone conversation. She gripped the edge of the counter, her knuckles white. "I got your email order for the gift shop yesterday, but I don't have it ready yet."

"Actually, I—"

Flavia's phone rang again. "I'm so sorry," she said. "I have to take this, but I see my clerk coming in the front door. Give her a second, and she can check you out."

Flavia disappeared behind the curtain as the door opened and a young woman dressed in jeans and a Candles and Curiosities Emporium T-shirt stepped inside. Quickly sizing up the situation, she hurried to stow her purse in the back then reappear at the register.

"Sorry about that. Flavia's been really preoccupied for the last few days."

Joy's brows rose. "Is that right?"

The young woman rang up the purchase then shrugged and handed Joy her bag. "Yeah, ever since someone came in the store talking about that angel statue going missing."

"Really?" Joy tried to sound casual as she took the bag.

"Yeah, but I understand why. She's an artist, so naturally she cares about works of art that are stolen."

"Yes, I can see that," Joy said. "That's perfectly understandable."

But was it?

They said their goodbyes, and Joy left the store and turned toward home.

Home.

How she loved that word. And the little place where she lived— the only place she'd lived alone in her life.

The first time Joy saw the sky-blue row house on Mercy Street, she fell in love with it. Situated on a lovely palm-lined street just a couple of blocks from Mercy Hospital and, of course, Rainbow Row, Joy adored almost everything about her peninsula house. Unlike her expansive, three-story residence located in a Houston suburb, this older, two-story house was perfect for her, with piazzas on each floor for her granddaughters to play to their hearts' content. And it was only a ten-minute walk to Charleston Harbor. A gated brick walkway led to the brand-new garage and a postage-stamp-sized walled-in yard that was just right for her gardening.

She was delighted with the small front yard that allowed her to dabble in her own landscaping without overwhelming her. She'd spent many a happy Saturday planning, planting, weeding, and trimming as she listened to audiobooks and podcasts.

The remodel of the inside—complete overhaul of the kitchen and bathrooms—was just about completed. Richard had just a few more small projects that he called "gilding the lily" to finish off before he would pronounce the job complete.

Joy stepped inside and deposited her keys and bag on the counter. After kicking off her shoes, she brewed a cup of tea. She'd come so close to speaking to Flavia.

Then an idea struck her. There was more than one way to hold a conversation with someone.

She picked up the phone and scrolled through her contacts until she reached the number for the store. With a press of a button, the phone rang.

"Candles & Curiosities Emporium. How can I help you?" a cheery voice said.

"It's Joy Atkins. Is this Flavia?"

"It is," the store owner said. "I'm so sorry our conversation was cut short. I had to answer that call. My brother can be persistent, and I hadn't seen him so worked up about a situation since he broke off his engagement ten years ago. I had to tell him to stop calling. Anyway, was there a problem with your purchase?"

"No, nothing like that," Joy said, "but I had hoped to speak with you about something important. Do you have a minute?"

Silence fell between them. Then Flavia answered. "Yes, of course. How can I help you?"

"My friend Evelyn saw two people in coveralls putting something into a van yesterday evening behind your building after the store was closed."

There was another moment of silence. "Did she say what it was?"

"She said it was big enough to be the angel statue and was wrapped in white cloth." Joy tried to keep her voice calm. "They put it in a van and backed down the alley in the opposite direction from where she was parked."

Again Flavia was quiet. Then she laughed. "Wait. What? You think I was harboring a stolen statue in my back room?"

"No, I mean ..." Joy paused a second too long.

"Oh, Joy. Hardly. But you're welcome to come and look around if that would make you feel better. Although I don't know what you'd be looking for, if they took the statue *out* of the building."

Joy wasn't going to pass up an opportunity to at least see if a statue could have been hidden in the store. "Great," she said brightly. "What about now?"

Silence.

"Flavia?"

"Sure, I'm at the studio, but I'll walk down and meet you in the alley. Just text when you're close. The studio is to the left of the store, down at the end of the row."

Joy hung up then scrolled through her contacts until she found Evelyn's name. She was about to place the call when she remembered that her friend would be at a lecture about now. And Anne would doubtless be occupied with spending time with her granddaughter.

Oh well. She'd go this one alone.

Joy put her cup in the sink and went to get her purse and keys. She'd just locked the back door and was heading to the garage when her phone rang.

"Hello, Sabrina," she said cheerily.

"Hey, Mom, can I ask a favor?"

"Name it." Joy stepped inside the garage then climbed into her car. With a press of the button, her garage door opened behind her.

"Sounds like you're going somewhere. Are you sure?"

"Sabrina," Joy said firmly. "What do you need?"

"Eloise bumped her chin on the playground, and we can't get it to stop bleeding. I called her pediatrician, and he advised that we take her to the emergency room to see if the wound needs a stitch."

"Oh no, the poor dear."

"She's actually handling it pretty well, but Mallory is beside herself worrying about her big sister, and wouldn't you know that Rob is out deep-sea fishing with some of his fraternity brothers. I can take Mallory with us to the emergency room, but ..."

"Nonsense," Joy said. "Yes, I was about to leave, but I can certainly take Mallory with me. Tell her Mimi will be there to pick her up in a few minutes."

"Thanks, Mom. You're the best."

When she arrived at Sabrina and Rob's house, she found Mallory watching for her out the front window. Joy had barely pulled the car to the curb when the front door opened and the little girl came racing out with the family dog, Mopsy, two steps behind her.

She wore a Wonder Woman T-shirt tucked into a pink tutu. On her feet were red galoshes dotted with yellow daisies and pink hearts. Not one to miss an opportunity to accessorize, Mallory had tucked a purple tiara dotted with multicolored rhinestones into her hair.

When Joy opened the door Mopsy edged past Mallory to help herself to the passenger seat. "You can't go, Mopsy," Mallory declared. "This is a Mimi and me day."

"Sorry, Mopsy," Joy said as she buckled Mallory into her booster seat. "Mallory is right."

Sabrina stepped onto the porch and waved. "Thanks, Mom."

"Is your dog part of the deal?" Joy called with a laugh.

"Definitely not," Sabrina said. "Mopsy, come."

The dog's ears lifted. Then she reluctantly jumped out of the Mini Cooper and raced back to Sabrina where she promptly showed her belly. Shaking her head, Sabrina knelt down to rub the dog's midsection as Joy drove away.

"Where are we going, Mimi?"

"On an adventure."

"Glorious!" her granddaughter exclaimed. Joy chuckled. Sabrina had informed her that was Mallory's new favorite word. "Now we need some music."

Joy obediently tuned the satellite radio in to Mallory's favorite station, and seconds later the little girl was singing along to the shark song that drove her mother batty. After a few minutes, they arrived at the shop on East Bay Street.

It was Saturday in the historic district, and parking spaces were at a premium. However, the alley was clear, and Joy was meeting Flavia behind her shop.

She clicked off the radio. This brought an immediate complaint from the back seat.

"See that alley right there?" She caught Mallory's attention in the rearview mirror. "We're about to go on another adventure. Are you ready?"

Mallory nodded. "Do I need to count one, two, three?"

"Sure," Joy said. "Start counting."

"One," Mallory announced. "Two."

She paused. Joy waited. "Mallory?"

"Just teasing, Mimi. Three."

At that, Joy turned into the alley and accelerated—only slightly, of course—until she reached the door marked with the address of Curiosities & Candles Emporium. By then, Mallory was giggling uncontrollably.

Joy looked up and down the alley. Up ahead she could see traffic going past on the next street. Here in the shadow of the centuries-old brick buildings, there were no cars and certainly no delivery vans in this block.

She reached for her phone and sent Flavia a text. A moment later, a heavy iron door opened at the other end of the block and the shopkeeper stepped outside into the alley.

Flavia's red hair was tucked up into a bun, and she wore a glittery yellow bandanna hairband. In contrast to her earlier outfit, she was wearing a pair of dark coveralls.

Chapter Ten

"THANK YOU FOR MEETING ME," Joy said when Flavia got near enough to speak. "I hope you don't mind, but I've brought my assistant."

Flavia's less-than-happy expression dissolved into a smile when she spied the little girl grinning at her from the back seat. "Well, look at you," she said. "Cool tiara."

"Thank you." Mallory studied Flavia for a moment. "I like yours too."

"Wanna trade?" Flavia asked.

Mallory nodded and handed over the tiara and accepted the bandanna. As Joy helped her put the hairband into place, Mallory leaned in and said, "That was Eloise's, so I didn't mind trading."

Though Joy was tempted to say something, their hostess—now sporting the purple tiara—had already unlocked the back door of the emporium and stepped inside. Joy locked the car and grasped Mallory's hand then followed Flavia into the store's back room.

Lights blazed on, temporarily blinding Joy. She blinked to adjust her eyes then found what was a fairly unremarkable room in front of her.

The center of the space was taken up by two primitive tables that looked as if they might each seat at least ten people. However, one of the tables appeared to be a catchall for everything from extra tape for the register to a basket full of newspapers and a set of keys on a massive silver ring. In contrast, the other table was bare. There were no chairs pulled up to either of them, but Joy did spy a stack of metal outdoor chairs under an old Dr Pepper clock that still lit up but did not appear to be keeping the correct time.

The walls to her right were lined with shelves that held everything from stacks of paper bags to boxes holding merchandise and other boxes marked Do Not Throw Away. Several artificial Christmas trees leaned together in the corner, their ornaments in boxes stacked next to them and marked on at least two sides.

To her left, Joy found a similar setup, only the boxes weren't marked. The place was organized chaos with all sorts of items being stored. Nothing in the space, however, gave her any hint that a statue had once been secreted there.

"Merchandise I'll put out eventually," Flavia said, guessing what Joy was wondering. "I've got more stuff than I'll ever be able to sell. But hey, at least I have a brother who's an architect and works for a construction company. I don't lack for shelves to store the things."

Joy glanced past the store's kitchen, which spanned the space directly behind where the cash register sat in the store. Then her eyes landed on another door. "Where does that go?"

"To my apartment." Flavia adjusted her tiara. "Have you seen what you wanted to see?"

There was that tone again. Not that Joy blamed her.

"Yes, thank you," she said. "I want you to understand, I'm just trying to be thorough. What with the theft of the statue—"

"Which I obviously did not take," Flavia supplied.

"No, of course not," Joy hurried to say, her voice gentle. "But I'm just following any lead. And since Evelyn was concerned about it, I had to check and see if there was any connection." She let out a long breath. "I've upset you. Will you forgive me? I'm just hoping to help a friend who shouldn't be blamed for the loss of our statue. In the process, I'm afraid I've overstepped the boundaries of friendship."

Flavia's expression softened. "I understand, and that's why I agreed to show you all of this. When I heard that someone took the statue, I have to say, I was mad. Really mad. I'm an artist, and if someone were to steal something I had done or something I owned, I would do whatever I could to get it back. Since you work at the hospital, you're one of the owners of the angel in a way, so I sort of feel a responsibility to help, you know?"

"Yes. I do feel like I have some kind of ownership in her." They were on the same side and wanted the same result. Joy would note that on her list as soon as she could manage it. "Thank you, Flavia."

"I mean, sculpting is such a difficult thing. To turn a rock into a person or a thing?" Flavia shook her head. "It's just so amazing. No matter how many times I've tried, my rock still looks like a rock when I'm done. It has to do with technique."

Flavia launched into a description of the process of using different sizes of chisels to attain a certain effect with the stone. All very interesting, and yet Joy couldn't see how any of it could be related to a missing statue.

Though she couldn't say she was any sort of sleuth, there was something bothering her about this situation. Something she couldn't let go of just yet. And her conversation with Coni the decorator was still fresh on her mind.

"Flavia, since you're active in the art community, can you think of anyone who might want to steal the statue? Someone who wants to make copies of it? Or maybe a collector who deals in that sort of thing?"

"Steal it?" Flavia laughed. "Um, no. But it did occur to me that an unscrupulous sculptor could have stolen the angel so the hospital would have to replace it, and then the thief would hope to get the commission. Probably half the sculptors I know would give anything to have one of their pieces on public display like that. Your work in a place of prominence for people to view for a couple of centuries? What idiot artist wouldn't jump at that chance? A legacy that lasts beyond your lifetime is a big deal. Also, there are people who just want a copy of something famous that's their very own. I've heard there are countless exact copies of the *Mona Lisa* hanging in homes all over the world. They know where the original is—but they don't care, see?"

Joy couldn't disagree. And she could see the logic in assuming that sort of legacy might be worth stealing to achieve.

"As to a collector who might want it stolen for them?" Flavia shrugged. "I'm sure they're out there, but anything to do with art pirates is out of my league."

Art pirates. An interesting term, and yet perhaps it fit. If someone took the Angel of Mercy and sold it to a private collector, wasn't that a form of piracy?

"What else do you do, Flavia?" Joy asked. "That is, what other kind of art do you make, I mean?"

Flavia adjusted her tiara again. "Lots of things. I did painting and screen printing in college, but lately I've settled on doing a few pieces of multimedia art. I've got a couple of things that will be in a gallery show soon, and I'm working on another one. Nothing I would sell in the shop, but I'm enjoying working on it. Want to see?"

"I would love to." Joy paused. "Just one more question first. I can't help noticing that you're wearing coveralls."

Flavia laughed. "Big step down from my usual attire in the store," she said.

"Well, it is different," Joy agreed. "But then, I guess I'm used to seeing you dressed in the latest fashion."

Flavia shrugged. "This is the latest fashion over at the studio. We all wear them."

"I see." Joy's mind was reeling with the possibilities, and her fingers itched to take notes. She pointed to Flavia's coveralls. "So do you buy these?" she asked as casually as she could manage.

"Oh no," Flavia said. "It comes with the studio rent. A uniform company delivers a whole bunch of them to us every two weeks. We dump our used ones into hampers that are picked up the same day the clean ones are delivered."

The sound of singing echoed in the room as Mallory burst out into the chorus of the shark song she loved so much. She had found a stack of papers and a pen on the table nearest to them and was busy creating her own art.

"It's a baby shark, Mimi," Mallory said when she realized she held the adults' attention.

"Honey, you should have asked before you started drawing on someone else's paper," Joy admonished.

Mallory's bottom lip went out. She dropped the pen but held tight to the paper.

A war of wills was about to begin. A war which every member of this child's immediate family, as well as several Sunday School and kindergarten teachers, were far too familiar with. Joy prepared to do battle.

"Cool shark," Flavia declared. "What's her name?"

Mallory peered up at the adult who'd surprised her but didn't loosen her grip on the treasure in her hand. "Baby."

Flavia studied the scribbled fish. "Want a frame for that?"

Mallory's eyes brightened. "Yes, please."

Apparently, Flavia Bowe was not only an expert at diffusing the ticking bomb that was a five-year-old, but she also brought out a level of politeness in her that usually required a reminder from a parent or grandparent. Joy gave Flavia a grateful smile.

Flavia held out her arm, and Mallory wrapped hers around it. Then she glanced over at Joy with a grin. "Coming with us, Mimi?"

"Absolutely."

Joy followed the pair out the door and down the alley, smiling as the shop owner and the five-year-old chattered back and forth about all things art. Gulls flew overhead, some of them alighting on the wires strung between two telephone poles.

Three doors down from the shop, Flavia paused to yank on a bell that hung outside a massive iron door coated in black paint and embellished with a single number: 8.

The door swung open on rusty hinges. "Follow right behind me," Flavia told them. "It's okay to look on the way, but don't touch, okay?"

Mallory nodded solemnly and held her paper to her chest. Joy also nodded her agreement.

The space that Flavia led them into was a high-ceilinged room with brick walls and floor-to-ceiling windows along the front and the back. Aisles had been made of plywood to section off spaces roughly the size of Joy's dining room for each artist while leaving the light from the windows streaming in.

The effect was not unlike the cubicles in the first office where Wilson worked right out of college. He used to joke that he was a worker bee in a hive back then. Of course, those worker bees never used blowtorches in their cubicles.

At least not that Wilson ever mentioned.

"It's noisy in here," Mallory complained. She screwed her face into a frown. "I don't like it."

"That's because people are working," Flavia said. "Don't you make noise when you work?"

Mallory giggled. Their conversation continued as they walked slowly down the aisles of the studio and Flavia patiently answered the five-year-old's questions. There were artists working on all kinds of projects, each in their own small cubicle. Joy fell behind Flavia and Mallory to get a better look at the jewelry, woodcarvings, paintings, etchings, and sculptures.

It was only after Joy rejoined the other two that she realized almost all the artists had been wearing dark coveralls. As was the glass artist who stopped working on a lovely vase to create a pink bubble for Mallory.

"Look, Mimi," Mallory said. "It's going to be a happy-thought bubble. I can put my happy thoughts in there so I will always have them."

Joy grinned. "How do you do that, sweetheart?"

"I just think them, and they go into the bubble." She nodded to the glassmaker. "That's what she said, and I believe her."

"Well, I believe her too." Joy shot a grateful smile toward the artist. "Thank you," she added when the piece was complete. "May I pay you for this?"

"No way," the young woman said. "I love kids. They're the true artists. They know exactly what they want. The rest of us spend our adult years trying to figure out what that is." She knelt to see Mallory eye to eye. "Your bubble has to finish cooling, but you can go ahead and start putting happy thoughts in it."

Flavia grinned at her friend. "We'll be back to collect the thought bubble on our way out. Thanks, Ace."

Mallory gave Ace a high five then marched away behind Flavia. Joy paused. "You have a gift with children," she said. "I really would like to pay for that. Or maybe purchase something from you?" She pointed to a lovely vase. "My name is Joy, by the way. Joy Atkins."

Ace shook her head. "Thank you, Mrs. Atkins. Pay it forward if you want. I've got all I need, and that vase is already going to a special home. My granny is in the Alzheimer's unit at Mercy Hospital, and there's a volunteer who comes and reads to her every day. Be someone else's blessing, and that'll be payment enough."

"I'll do that, Ace."

Joy walked past sculptors chipping away at stone and painters leaning over their easels, some with music blaring and some working in silence. Or rather whatever silence they could manage amid the noise.

In the space in the corner where the windows facing the street met the side wall, Flavia stopped. Peering inside, Joy could see an easel set up beside a small table overflowing with paints, brushes, and rags in the middle of the sunny little room.

"Okay, kiddo," she told Mallory. "This is where I paint my pictures. But guess what?"

"What?" Mallory asked, tugging at the bandanna that had worked its way down toward her brows. Joy adjusted the cloth back into place as Mallory watched their hostess attentively.

"I also make my frames here. At least it's quieter right now." She nodded toward the wooden wall separating her space from the one next door. "It looks like my neighbor is taking a break."

Flavia moved quickly to the table and scooped up enough of the items there to allow a small amount of space. Depositing the brushes and paints on the nearest shelf, one of dozens lining the brick outside wall and the smaller wooden wall opposite it, she retrieved four small pieces of driftwood and carried them to the table.

"What about these for the frame? I got them from the beach."

"I like the beach," Mallory said. "So yes."

While Joy and Mallory watched, Flavia turned the pieces of driftwood into a lovely little frame for the shark picture. "It needs something," Flavia proclaimed. "Don't you think?"

"Sparkles," Mallory said.

Flavia nodded. "Sparkles," she agreed, and then she looked up at Joy. "Mimi, do we have time to put sparkles on this frame? Maybe while you look around?"

Her meaning was impossible to miss. "I think that's a grand idea. Do you mind, Mallory? I'll be close by. Or I can wait here until you're done, if you prefer."

Mallory shook her head. "I'll be here making my frame sparkle."

"I won't be long," Joy told them, but both artists had their heads already bent over their project.

Her first stop was back on the aisle where she'd seen a sculptor chipping away at a block of marble. Unlike the others who wore the coveralls provided by the landlord, this artist was dressed in a denim shirt and pants with what looked like a construction worker's tool belt slung low on his hips. A pair of heavy work boots and heavy leather gloves more fitting to a job site than an art studio completed his attire.

Everything, including his honey-colored beard and close-cropped hair, was covered with a fine dusting of marble. Joy watched from a distance until he caught sight of her. Then she drew near.

"Am I bothering you?" she asked.

"A bit," he admitted. "I'm not used to being watched while I work."

His tone was terse, and his accent was one of a local. He studied her closely, his eyes a striking green, as he swung an oversized wooden mallet with his left hand. At this moment, the sculptor looked more like a burly blacksmith or a linebacker who had been given the wrong uniform.

She offered a smile in hopes it would placate him. "I'm fascinated at how you know where to chip away and where to leave it as it is."

The sculptor swiped at his brow with the back of his hand, leaving a trail of marble dust behind. "The sculpture is already complete within the marble block before I start my work. It's already there. I just have to chisel away the superfluous material."

"Oh." She took in his words as she looked at the lump of marble. "That's such a beautiful way to put it."

"Yeah, well, I thought so too. Actually, Michelangelo said it, but I can't disagree."

"Do you do this full-time?" When he frowned, she hurried to add, "Sculpt, I mean. Not steal quotes from Michelangelo."

He seemed poised to respond in a manner that fit his irritated expression. Then, by degrees, a smile arose. To Joy's surprise, the smile became laughter.

"No to both," he said when only remnants of a grin remained. "I sculpt on weekends when I'm not working overtime at my construction job, and I only know one Michelangelo quote, so neither pays the bills or the rent on this space."

"I'm Joy Atkins," she told him. "I'm here as a guest of Flavia Bowe. She and my granddaughter are currently embellishing a frame over in Flavia's space."

The big man looked as if he might not respond. Then he removed a glove and closed the distance to shake her hand. "Colin Guest. Pleased to meet you, Mrs. Atkins."

"Claudia's son?" she said, searching his face for any resemblance.

"Nephew," he said, withdrawing his hand and looking displeased.

Joy realized her smile had faltered and propped it up again. "Your aunt is a neighbor of mine. I purchased a house on Mercy

Street six months ago. She was one of the first neighbors I met after I moved in."

"Yeah, that figures. Aunt Claudia is a social butterfly." He said the words in a tone that told her he either didn't approve or just plain didn't like it.

"Actually, I saw her this morning at the garden club meeting."

Her attempt at making conversation was a dismal failure. Colin snatched up his chisel and turned back to his work. "That's nice," he said as he plunged the chisel into the marble then hit it with the mallet.

"Colin, can I ask you a question?"

He froze but made no move to look at her. "As long as it doesn't relate to my family, sure."

"What do you know about the Angel of Mercy statue?"

Colin turned around to face Joy. "That's a broad question. Are you asking me about the history of it, the making of it, or the location of it? All very different answers."

"Okay," she said forcing herself not to cower under his superior height and angry scowl. "I know the first, wouldn't have a clue what to do with the information if you told me the second, but I am very interested in hearing the answer to the third."

"You and a whole lot of people," he quipped.

"You know she's been stolen."

His scowl slipped just a bit. "You can't live in Charleston without knowing that. And you can't be related to Claudia Guest without having to hear about it on repeat. Are you a cop?"

Chapter Eleven

THE SWIFTNESS WITH WHICH HE changed the direction of the subject surprised Joy. "Goodness, no," she said. "Although, I would like very much to help the police find it. Honestly, I'd prefer to see it returned even if we never find out who took it. You see, I manage the gift shop at Mercy Hospital, and I'm just a plain ol' grandmother. Colin, as I understand it, the Angel of Mercy was carved by your ancestor. I'd think you'd want it found for personal reasons yourself."

"I doubt the police agree with you regarding the capture of the thief. They like to have someone to lock up when a crime has been committed."

She shook her head. "I don't care if they agree. I just want the angel to come home. I miss walking past it every morning on my way to open the gift shop." Joy held his gaze, refusing to look away. "Look," she said, "all I want is to find the statue and return it, and if you know anything about it, I'd appreciate it if you told me."

He frowned. "What makes you think I know anything?"

Joy shrugged. "I don't know. But if you see or hear anything, I'm at the gift shop at Mercy Hospital weekdays from about six forty-five a.m. on. I've always got a pot of coffee and a listening ear ready to go. One more thing. Did you see anything unusual here last night?"

Colin stared at her a moment longer. "I would ask you to define unusual, but considering these are artists, that's a tall order. Regardless, no, I did not."

He turned back to his work. Joy was just about to step away when he glanced over his shoulder. "I'll keep what you said in mind. Right now, there's just one thing I've got to say about that missing statue."

"I'm listening," she told him.

"Have you considered it's not about the statue?"

She shook her head. "What do you mean?"

"Think about it, Mrs. Atkins."

"I don't understand," Joy said.

Instead of elaborating, Colin reached over to turn on a speaker that immediately blasted heavy metal music at high volume. Then he went back to his work on the block of marble.

It didn't take a fool to know that this conversation was most definitely over. And Joy was no fool.

Moving past empty spaces, Joy stopped at the next occupied studio, where she found a woman about her age seated in front of an easel. Though she couldn't see what the artist was working on, she couldn't miss the concentration on the woman's face.

She also couldn't help but notice that this woman too hadn't donned the coveralls that were provided with the rent. Instead, she sported a pair of paint-splattered overalls over a white short-sleeved T-shirt. Her silver hair was pulled back into a chignon at the base of her neck, and her eyes were bright blue.

"Excuse me," Joy said. "May I interrupt you for a moment?"

The woman startled then quickly recovered. "Oh, hello. Sure. I'm not accomplishing much anyway." She stood and came over to the door. "How can I help?"

"I'm Joy Atkins," Joy said.

"I know you," the woman responded. "You manage the gift shop at Mercy Hospital."

"Yes, that's right."

The woman leaned against the doorframe, her hands clasped in front of her. "As I recall, you serve the best coffee in Charleston. If I weren't intent on never seeing the inside of that hospital or their breast cancer wing again, I'd come back to visit just because of the coffee."

Joy wasn't sure how to respond to that, so she said, "I always keep a pot ready for visitors, and you're welcome anytime."

As if she recalled something she forgot, the woman shook her head. "I'm sorry. I haven't introduced myself, Joy. I'm Leah Ainsworth."

"Pleased to meet you, Leah. I'm curious—are you related to India Ainsworth-Brown?"

"I'm afraid so. I'm her sister. But before you ask, no, I don't grow roses, nor do I have a green thumb of any sort. I pay a gardener good money to make it look like I do though." She chuckled. "Don't tell India that. She thinks I have a talent for growing things. She has no idea I purchase that talent by the hour and am most grateful that I don't have to know anything other than how to write the check at the end of the month."

Joy allowed the woman's previous statement about the breast cancer wing to sink in. "I'm sorry about your experience with breast cancer. It's a terrible thing. I lost my mother to it."

"Yes," Leah said softly. "It is, and I hate that you've lost your mother to it. But I'm in remission, and that's a blessing." She shook her head again. "No, it's not the cancer that was the problem. It was the hospital."

Joy frowned. "Oh. Did something happen?"

Leah leveled her an even gaze. "How much time have you got? A lot of things happened, and none of them were good. From the minute I went under the knife until the day I was finally released, it was one calamity after the other. I would sue, but my lawyers say the case isn't that easy to prove. I know what happened, but a doctor has a whole hospital behind him."

"Well, that can be true, but—"

"And at the head of all that is the administrator," Leah said, interrupting. "He's the one who called and told me that as much as he regretted it—off the record, mind you—their insurance policies wouldn't be paying anything to settle my matter out of court." She paused. "I'm sorry. I shouldn't have unloaded on you. It's not like you were the doctor on call when I came in and needed emergency surgery. That honor belongs to Chad Barnhardt."

Joy kept her expression neutral. "Again, I'm sorry."

Leah swiped at the air as if erasing the negativity around her. "No, again, I'm the one who's sorry. You came to me, and I asked how I could help then dumped all this on you. I blame Chad Barnhardt and the hospital management, not you. Let's start over." She stuck her hand out and shook Joy's in a firm grip. "I'm Leah Ainsworth. How can I help you?"

Joy smiled. "I'm asking the artists who work here if they saw anything unusual last night. I'm thinking of someone who might have brought in what looked like a mummy between, say, eight and nine o'clock."

Leah shook her head. "Can't help you. Believe it or not, I was actually on a date. I know. At my age. I never thought I would date after I lost my husband, but here I am. And you know what?"

"What?" Joy said.

"I'm actually having fun."

All she could manage was a nod. Sabrina had tried her best to convince Joy to consider dipping her toe into the dating pool. *"Dad didn't want you to spend the rest of your life alone, Mom. He told me himself."*

Wilson had told her too. More than once. Trouble was, Joy wasn't about to listen to it at the time. Nor was she ready to hear it now.

"Well, good for you," Joy said brightly, and she found she meant it. Just because she wasn't quite ready for male companionship, that didn't mean other widows shouldn't seek it.

"I'm looking into the theft of the Angel of Mercy statue," Joy told her, shrugging off the topic for a safer one. "I'm not working for the police, but I am hoping to help them. So, one last question: Is there anything you know that might help me with that?"

"Nothing that hasn't been written in the papers or reported on television," Leah said. "I may be an amateur artist, but I have absolutely no connection to the art world." She paused. "Or, for that matter, the art-theft world."

It took a moment to see that Leah was teasing. "Right," Joy said. "Well, the offer for coffee stands."

Leah smiled. "Thank you. I just might take you up on that."

Joy found her way back to Mallory and Flavia. She didn't bother to speak with any of the other artists. She'd done enough sleuthing to satisfy her for now.

She'd also seen enough to know that almost anything could have been under that white cloth. However, it was hard to imagine how someone could have safely hidden the statue in this place. After all, there were no closets or storage spaces in these studios, and little to no privacy. Just blank walls and an opening cut for a door. A few of the studios did have curtains hung across the openings, but none was closed completely.

Still, Joy had learned plenty. Claudia Guest's nephew was an artist who spent time here. That was a connection to the statue, even though it might be a distant one.

She returned to find Mallory and Flavia wrapping up their project. Though Mallory wore as much glitter as she'd put on her frame, she beamed from ear to ear.

"Look, Mimi, isn't it fabulous?"

"Fabulous? Is that your new favorite word?"

Mallory nodded.

"Thank you," Joy said to Flavia. "You've made her day."

Mallory looked up at Flavia and beamed. "Thank you, Miss Flavia," she said, once again without prompting.

"You are very welcome. Would you like your crown back?" Flavia asked.

"You may keep it if you'd like," Mallory said.

Flavia appeared to consider the idea. Then she shrugged. "I don't have a place for a crown here. I'm afraid it might get broken. I wonder if you'd help me out with that."

"I could keep it for you at my house," Mallory said.

"That would be wonderful." She removed the crown and handed it to Mallory. "And keep the bandanna too. It looks better on you than it ever did on me."

Mallory tucked the tiara on top of her bandanna. "I'll take care of it, but I may have to share it with my sister, Eloise. She's nine and bossy, and the tiara's kind of hers."

"Then it's very good that it will stay at your house." Flavia somehow managed to keep a straight face as she bid them goodbye.

"I'll let you know if I hear anything," she called after them.

"That would be great. Thank you," Joy said.

They got all the way to the car before Joy realized that Mallory was crying. She scooped the little girl into her arms.

"Honey, it's okay. I promise we'll go back and see Miss Flavia again."

Her granddaughter looked up into Joy's eyes, tears now staining her cheeks. "That's not it," she managed.

"Then what is it?"

"I'm sad about Eloise."

"Because you took her crown?"

She shook her head. "No, because she got hurt. Can we go see her?"

Joy gave her a squeeze. "We'll see her soon, I promise."

"Can we see her now?"

Joy glanced down at her shirt. "Not like we're dressed right now." Mallory's lower lip went out, and Joy hurried to add. "It's nothing a bath won't fix."

The lower lip quavered. Mallory's dislike of baths was just one of her current quirks.

"Is it a rule?"

Joy nodded. "Or we can go back to Mimi's house and dig in the dirt."

Mallory's smile returned, and the decision was made.

A few hours later, Sabrina arrived to pick up her youngest daughter.

"Where's Eloise?" Mallory demanded, dirt crumbling from her hands as she hurried to hug her mother.

"She's home with Daddy." Sabrina looked past Mallory to Joy. "He got home a few minutes ago. No stitches for Eloise. She just has to keep the bandage on for a few days."

"That's good news."

"Let's go home, Mommy," Mallory said. "Mimi and I had an adventure, and I made a picture." She paused. "And Miss Flavia and I made a frame. It's fabulous."

"Flavia?" Sabrina asked.

"Flavia Bowe." Joy shook her head. "It's a long story. Can I call you later?"

"Sure." Sabrina herded her daughter out to the car then waited while Mallory buckled herself in. "You were brave to take this one to Curiosities & Candles Emporium."

"Actually, we only met up with Flavia. There was no shopping involved." Joy paused. "I've been looking into the disappearance of the Angel of Mercy statue, and one of the possible clues led to the alley behind Flavia's store."

Sabrina looked at Joy as if she'd lost her mind. "What?"

"Are you surprised that I might be doing a little investigating?" Joy chuckled. "Well, I am too. But I'm just looking into it on behalf of a friend. Plus, I miss seeing the angel. She should come back home."

"Well, I do agree about all that. I'm just surprised that you're the one doing the investigating. Why not the police? Have they dropped the case already?"

"Oh no. At least, I don't think so." Joy was beginning to regret mentioning this to her daughter.

"Mommy," came the insistent voice from the back seat. "Let's go. And I want to hear the shark song."

Sabrina rolled her eyes. "I hate that song," she whispered to Joy.

"I heard you," Mallory called. "Mimi doesn't hate that song. Mimi lets me hear it over and over as many times as I want."

Joy shrugged then upped her grin. Their former topic forgotten, Sabrina climbed into her SUV and closed the door then said something to Mallory. Likely the battle for the radio was about to begin.

As soon as she bid goodbye to Sabrina and Mallory, Joy headed for the shower. Afterward she spent time writing down all her impressions of the afternoon. When she was done, she read over everything, stopping to underline the question Colin Guest had asked.

"Have you considered it's not about the statue?"

She tapped her pencil against the surface of her desk and thought about that question. "What did you mean by that, I wonder?" she said aloud.

She dug the grocery list turned suspect list out of her purse. She inserted Colin Guest as her first entry, based as much on his attitude about the statue as his attitude about his mother.

Then came Leah Ainsworth. She was angry at Dr. Barnhardt and the hospital administration, and she had made that abundantly clear. Also, she was an artist and, whether or not she wanted to admit it, she did have connections in that world.

Joy thought of the other woman she and Mallory had met at the studio. Her name was Ace, but other than the fact she was a glass-blower whose grandmother had been a patient in Mercy Hospital's Alzheimer's unit, that was all Joy knew about her.

"I should have asked more questions," Joy muttered, feeling like the novice investigator she was. At least she knew where she could find Ace if there was a need to contact her again.

Her eyes traveled back up the list to the place where she had written Flavia's name. Again she tapped the end of the pen on her desk.

Flavia had been helpful and completely transparent in allowing Joy access to not only her studio space but also the back room of her store. She had answered questions and treated Mallory like an honored guest.

Everything in Joy's heart said that Flavia was not involved in anything related to the missing statue. Still acutely aware that she had much to learn in the way of sleuthing, Joy left her on the list. She did, however, place a question mark next to her name.

That done, Joy pressed back from her desk and stretched her arms then her neck. She picked up the novel she'd been reading and made another glass of iced tea. Instead of settling on the piazza, Joy took her book and tea to her small garden, to the bench that she'd brought from Houston.

It had taken Wilson more than a year to make the bench, and when he was done Joy would have sworn that all four legs were a different length. It was an early piece, he would claim later, and needed to be updated.

But Joy wouldn't hear of it. She liked the bench just the way it was, even if she did have to stack small pieces of wood under the three shortest legs to even things out.

Her phone dinged with a text, and Joy snatched it up. It was Anne. HAVE YOU BEEN ENJOYING A QUIET AFTERNOON?

Joy chuckled. IT'S BEEN INTERESTING. WANT TO SEE MY NOTES?

Anne's response was swift. OF COURSE! TAKE PICTURES OF THEM AND SEND THEM TO ME.

Joy sent photos then added one more comment. LET'S CHAT MORE ON MONDAY. I WOULD LIKE TO HEAR YOUR THOUGHTS.

DEFINITELY, Anne wrote back. AND WOW! YOU WERE BUSY! MIND IF I SEND ALL OF THIS TO EVELYN TO CATCH HER UP?

PLEASE DO. I'M UNPLUGGING TONIGHT AND TOMORROW. SEE YOU ON MONDAY.

While she had the phone in her hand, Joy quickly texted Sabrina to check on Eloise and Mallory once more.

TOLD MALLORY IF SHE WANTED TO LISTEN TO THE SHARK SONG SHE'D HAVE TO GO WITH ELOISE UP TO THE PLAYROOM. THEY'VE BEEN UP THERE FOR AN HOUR. ALL IS WELL, FAR AS I CAN TELL. LOVE YOU, MOM.

Joy responded then tucked her phone into her pocket and rose. Time to do something else before it got too dark and she had to go inside. She took one more glance around the garden and then stepped into the small room attached to the garage. She'd told Richard what she wanted the room for, and after asking her a dozen questions, he'd designed a space that fulfilled her every wish.

Her son-in-law had set up a grow light for her above her workbench, and she was very pleased with the arrangement. With the addition of the special light, she could manage the conditions that delicate seedlings needed to flourish.

Conditions that delicate roses needed to root and bloom.

Joy smiled as she beheld her latest treasure to her patch of abundance. There in all its glory was the unmistakable bud of a cream-colored Noisette rose.

And if she looked closely, Joy could see just a hint of the crimson at its center.

"Oh my goodness!"

She'd done it. Joy had propagated the very rose that Dr. Claudia Guest, an expert in Charleston Noisette roses, had publicly proclaimed could not possibly exist.

Now what?

There was no point in informing Detective Osborne about something so inconsequential as a bud on a rosebush. Still, Joy took a moment to admire the tiny bud before stepping back outside and locking the door behind her.

The grow light would do its work, and the bloom would flourish. Then Joy just might tell someone about the treasure she'd managed to cultivate.

Chapter Twelve

On Monday morning Joy walked past the gift shop, pausing only long enough to make sure that the arrangements she'd hastily made with her volunteer had worked out. Indeed, Lacy Vincent was standing behind the counter alongside Angela, who'd agreed to come in early today.

Waving through the glass door, Joy continued on to the ornate elevators and pressed the button for the top floor where the administrative offices were. Once there, she took a seat on a bench in view of the elevator and waited.

Only then did Joy decide she probably should have brought a mug of coffee with her. She stood, thinking she would hurry downstairs and grab a cup.

Unfortunately, the elevator doors opened, and Garrison Baker stepped out. "Joy," he exclaimed. "This is a surprise. When you weren't in the gift shop, I thought maybe you were out today."

She looked down at his hand and saw he was carrying a mug.

Garrison held it up. "Your volunteer said it would be okay. I promised her I would see that the mug was returned by the end of the day."

Joy waved away the comment. "You're the administrator. I think it'll be fine."

He laughed and then quickly sobered. "This isn't an accidental meeting, is it?"

"No," Joy admitted. "I knew you tend to arrive before the rest of the folks up here. I thought maybe I could convince you to give me a few minutes of your time. It won't take long."

He paused only a moment before nodding. "Sure. Come on."

Garrison led her down a carpeted hallway then opened the doors leading to his office. "Come on in and have a seat."

The administrator's office was relatively unchanged since the days when Henry Sanchez occupied the space. From the massive desk, piled high with papers, to the credenza and bookshelves behind him, and the gold-framed maps and paintings of Mercy Hospital through the years, the office left no doubt that it belonged to the man who ran things around here.

Joy settled onto a chair across the desk from Garrison and waited until he nodded in her direction. "Okay," he said as he took a sip from the mug that bore the Mercy Hospital logo, "what can I do for you?" He shook his head. "Keeping in mind I can probably help with just about anything except increasing your budget."

"This isn't about the budget," she assured him.

"Well, that's a relief. Nine out of ten people who sit in that chair come to my office to tell me why their department needs more money. And the trouble is, most of them are absolutely right. Anyway, again, what can I do for you?"

"It's about the Angel of Mercy statue," she said. "Have there been any updates since Friday? There's been nothing on the news about it nor on the internet. Just the report from last week."

Garrison let out a long breath. "I wish there were, but no. There's been nothing new."

"I'm sorry to hear that."

Joy paused. Though she'd thought carefully about how she would present her request for information, now that she was seated across the desk from the hospital administrator, she decided to go the direct route.

"Were there any witnesses to the theft of the statue?"

He barely blinked. "On the record?"

"It doesn't have to be."

"Okay, then. Off the record, yes. There was. Norm Ashford has given a statement."

"Norm?"

Joy recalled the security guard who was always happy to fix his own coffee and never let her open a door on her own if he was anywhere nearby. The fellow who always left the gift shop with a tip of his hat.

"Why isn't this information being reported on?"

"Because the police have decided not to release everything to the public yet. That's all I know."

She nodded. "Yes, I suppose keeping something to themselves gives the police the upper hand."

"Was that all you wanted to know?"

"Almost." Joy met his gaze. "Just so I'm clear, the police only have one witness, and that's Norm. There are no others?"

"There are plenty of people who have spoken to them, most of them employees of the hospital or patients. Some are visitors. But unless the police are withholding information from me, then yes, Norm is the only witness."

Joy moved to the edge of her seat but wasn't quite ready to go just yet. "What did Norm see?"

Garrison shook his head. "That I can't tell you." He shrugged. "Sorry, but even off the record there's only so much I'm allowed to say."

"And is Norm allowed to talk about what he saw?"

"I don't know what instructions Norm was given," he said. "I wasn't there when the police met with him." Garrison's phone rang. "And so it begins. Welcome to Monday."

"Yes, I've taken up plenty of your time." Joy stood. "Thank you."

He answered his phone as she reached the door, and she heard him ask the caller to hold. "Joy," he said, and she turned around to look back in his direction, "I've trusted you with this information."

"And I won't betray that trust," she said. "Though I may pay Norm a visit."

"I thought you would. I would appreciate it if you didn't mention to him where you got your information."

"I promise," she said.

He seemed to be studying her. "Are you investigating this theft? Unofficially, I mean? Or are you just curious?"

She moved a few steps closer. "My friends and I are investigating. That would be Anne Mabry and Evelyn Perry. Do you mind if I tell them about Norm?"

Garrison frowned. "If you think they can be trusted," he said. "Just please keep in mind what I've told you."

"Of course."

The phone buzzed, a reminder that a call was on hold. "Oh, one more thing. If you see Nurse Bashore, please thank her for her recommendation. I enjoyed church yesterday."

"I'll do that," she said with a smile that lasted all the way back down to the gift shop.

Joy found Lacy assisting a customer and busied herself arranging the books on the shelf nearest the front window. When the customer was gone, she walked over to the counter.

"Everything going okay this morning?"

"Going great," Lacy said. "Angela has been making the deliveries this morning while I mind the shop."

"Good. I've got an errand to run. Do you mind staying a little while longer?"

"No, go on," Lacy said. "It's fine."

Lacy had been with Joy longer than any of the other volunteers, and she'd always been a reliable and able assistant. "All right. I won't be long."

Joy snatched up her purse from the back and shrugged it over her shoulder. She saw Lacy looking at her phone but chose to ignore it. In general, she preferred that her employees stay off their phones while customers were in the shop. However, to be fair, the place was empty.

The young woman looked up. "Big news, Mrs. Atkins," she said.

"Oh? Have they found the statue?"

"No," she said. "But there's a hurricane in the Atlantic. Right now they've got us right in its path."

"Great," Joy said. "Let's hope it makes a turn and moves offshore where it won't bother anyone."

"Might be possible but not likely. My update says it'll make landfall by the end of the week." She looked up once again, this time with a smile. "And guess what the name is?"

"I give up," Joy said, her hand now on the doorknob.

"Joy. She's only a tropical storm right now, but when she gets to Charleston, she'll be Hurricane Joy."

Joy groaned and left without responding. Instead of heading toward the exit, she turned and walked to the records department where she found Evelyn seated at her desk, her fingers tapping a quick rhythm on her keyboard.

Joy knocked twice then waited for Evelyn to look her way. "Come in," she said when she'd finished her typing. "I didn't think I'd see you so early today."

"Neither did I." Joy glanced around and shut the door. "Have you got a minute? I've got something I want to discuss, and I'm under instructions not to let the word get out beyond the three of us."

"Sure, go ahead," Evelyn said, swiveling in her chair. "What's up?"

Joy told Evelyn about her visit to Garrison Baker and how someone needed to talk to Norm, who wasn't scheduled to work today.

"So you want reinforcements?" Evelyn said with a chuckle. She checked her watch. "I stayed late three days last week, so I can take a few minutes this morning."

"I'd really appreciate that. The three of us are working on this together, so technically I'm here to ask if you want to come with me to interview a witness to the theft." She shrugged. "I also wondered if you could drive."

Evelyn nodded. "Let me look at my calendar to make sure nothing has popped up since I reviewed it on Friday." She navigated to her calendar and clicked a few buttons. Then she pushed away from her desk and reached into the bottom desk drawer on the left for her purse and keys.

Ten minutes later, they were parked outside Norm's modest bungalow. "You're sure this is the place?" Evelyn asked her.

"I hope so," Joy said. "It's the address that was in the old hospital address book back when they published those things. Unless he's moved." She shook her head. "I think the copy I found at the thrift store was from the nineties. Anyway, unless he's moved, it should be his place."

"Why in the world did you buy an old hospital address book at a thrift store?" Evelyn asked as she turned off the engine and stepped out of her car.

"I got it in a bundle of telephone books that I was going to take apart and use for mulch in my garden. When I saw what it was, I couldn't tear it up." She beamed. "And see, I was right. It finally has been useful."

"Let's hope so." Evelyn walked up to the door with Joy following behind.

Norm answered the door, and shock registered on his face. He was dressed in khakis and a purple polo and a pair of white sneakers. "To what do I owe this visit, ladies?"

"Do you have a minute?" Evelyn asked.

"I was on my way out to play a round of golf. It's my day off, you know."

"Maybe we could talk to you on your way to your car?" Joy suggested.

"Since my car's right there, it would be a short conversation." He sighed. "But I can spare a few minutes. What's going on?"

"You were a witness to the theft of the Angel of Mercy statue," Joy said.

Norm grimaced then shook his head. "So the news got out?"

"No," Joy told him. "I was given the information in confidence because Evelyn and I—and our friend Anne—are looking to uncover the facts surrounding the disappearance."

"I suppose it won't hurt." He nodded toward the black sedan in his driveway. "That doesn't change the fact that I've got a tee time coming up."

"Understood," Joy said. "Can you just tell us what you saw? I'll take notes, and Evelyn, why don't you ask any questions that occur to you?" She paused. "We'll be quick. I promise."

"If that's all you want to know, it won't take long. I saw a black pickup parked next to the curb on the side of the building. Underneath that big magnolia. Engine was running but no lights on and no one in it. That was the first thing that caught my attention. Then there was another vehicle in the back. Nothing that ought to have been there at that hour."

Joy's ears perked up. "What kind of vehicle? Did you get a plate number on either of them?"

"Couldn't see that well. The plates were covered with dirt, and it was dark out. I noted it in my report. I believe the time was something like a quarter to three." He nodded. "Yes, that was it exactly."

"So, the other vehicle. Was it a pickup too? A van? Something bigger?"

"It was a heavy-duty pickup, also black, pulling a flatbed trailer with a front loader on it."

"A front loader?" Evelyn said.

"A small tractor with an attachment on the front," he explained. "Useful in gardening, but I suspect it might have ended up being how the crooks got away with the statue."

"How so?" Evelyn asked. "Are you saying that whoever took the statue used a tractor to lift it onto a flatbed trailer?"

"That's how I figure it. Our angel was almost life-size but not very tall, maybe four and a half feet or so. By the way, it's not difficult to remove a stone statue from a metal base. Four metal screws held her in place. That's all."

"I didn't know that," Evelyn said. "I guess I thought it would be more securely fastened."

"It worked fine until someone tampered with it. Remember, she withstood Union fire and more hurricanes than we can count, and there she still stood."

"Until Wednesday morning," Joy said.

"Yes, that's right," Norm said.

"Could the pickups, the flatbed trailer, and front loader have belonged to gardeners?" Evelyn suggested.

"They could have," he said, "but not our gardeners. We employ ours in-house, and I've got a log of all vehicles. That one isn't on it." He shook his head. "I should clarify that. The hospital does not own a vehicle of that type. I made sure to confirm it."

Evelyn gave Joy a sideways look then returned her attention to Norm. "Who did you confirm that with?"

"The boss man, of course. Anytime I see something unusual, procedure is to call Garrison Baker." Norm checked his watch. "Is that all? I've got about two minutes and then I've got to go."

"I've got a question," Joy said. "Did you see anything in the front of the building?"

"Not part of my normal patrol," he said.

"Why not?" Evelyn asked.

He shrugged. "There aren't cameras in the back yet," he said. "So we make that area part of our exterior patrol. But the front has cameras."

"Right."

"Just one more question," Evelyn said. "What happened to the vehicles?"

"I went inside to do my rounds thinking someone would be called out to check on it. That's protocol in these cases. They don't want a guard stuck in one place when he's supposed to be patrolling certain areas at certain times. So another guard is on call to handle any incident that happens, leaving the guard on duty to keep to his rounds. But to answer your question, when I went back out there, everything was gone."

"So you don't know whether anyone checked on it."

"Oh, I know," he said. "No one was called out, so the answer is no."

Joy looked up at Norm. "Mr. Baker didn't call anyone out?"

"Nope."

"You're certain."

"There are seven guards in the department. We all shift between days, evenings, and nights, and one day a week we are each on call for incidents like this. The man who was on call wasn't called." He moved toward his car. "I can give you his name, but he'll tell you what I've just told you."

"No, that isn't necessary." Evelyn looked over at Joy. "Anything else?"

"No, let's let Norm get to his golf game." Joy smiled at the guard. "Thank you for your help. If you think of anything else, will you let us know?"

"You bet I will," Norm said. "Wouldn't want to let down the lady who sees I've always got good coffee whenever I want it."

Joy followed Evelyn back to her car then slipped inside and buckled her seat belt. "Did you get all of that?" Evelyn asked once they were on their way back to the hospital.

"I think so. I wish he'd stuck around to see who drove those vehicles away."

"Me too." Evelyn signaled to turn then glanced over at Joy. "Are you as bothered as I am that Garrison Baker didn't place that call to send a security guard out to investigate?"

"What do you make of that?" Joy asked her.

"Well," Evelyn said slowly, "there's a budget crisis going on at the hospital right now."

There was no need to finish that thought. Joy knew where she was going with it.

And try as she might, she couldn't disagree.

Retrieving her notebook, Joy turned to the list of witnesses she'd been compiling. Beneath the last name on the list, she wrote one more.

GARRISON BAKER.

Chapter Thirteen

JOY WALKED WITH EVELYN ACROSS the parking lot and stopped at the sidewalk leading inside the building. "I'm sorry, I have to go back in," Evelyn said. "I've got a meeting in thirty minutes, and I need to prepare for it."

"We'll talk later. I think Anne is working this morning. Or maybe it's this afternoon. In any case, let's compare notes when we get a chance."

Evelyn consulted her watch. "Okay, I'm off."

Joy waved goodbye to her friend then walked on the sidewalk around the hospital to the side, under the magnolia tree where Norm had seen the trucks. Though she saw several marks that might have been made by tires, there was nothing unusual about them. It wasn't unusual to see maintenance vehicles on the hospital lawn.

Then she turned her attention to the hospital. There was a five-foot decorative hedge that ran about two feet away from and all the way down the brick wall since there were no first-floor windows on this side.

She set off in a straight line from the place where she was standing and walked toward the building. A sidewalk took her most of the way before it ended in another walkway parallel to the building that forced her to go either to the left and around to the front of the hospital, or to the right, to the back of the building, which was the harbor side.

Joy went to the statue base and examined the ground around it. The thief—or *thieves* as she now considered since there were two vehicles—would have driven the front loader to here and then back to the pickup. But there were no tire tracks or ruts marring the immaculate green carpet anywhere. So was the front loader used to move the statue or not?

Joy walked back inside more confused than ever. Just as she reached the gift shop, her phone rang. Though she didn't recognize the number, she answered it.

"Joy, this is Norm. The woman who answered the phone at the gift shop gave me your number."

Joy sighed. There would be a lesson on giving out cell phone numbers when she had a moment with her volunteers. At least this time it turned out okay.

"I need to talk to you," he continued. "But not at the hospital."

"I thought you were playing golf."

"I was," he said. "But this weighed on me, and I couldn't end up hitting anywhere close to par. I gave up on the fourth hole and called it a day. Can you meet me at the Cathedral of St. John the Baptist on Broad Street? I'll be waiting for you there."

She saw Lacy and Angela watching her and waved. "Where?"

"I'll watch for you," was his answer.

"Okay, when?"

"Now would be good."

Joy swallowed hard. At this point she wouldn't get any work done. But she could hardly miss this opportunity.

"Evelyn will be in a meeting about now," she said.

"That's fine," he told her. "I'd rather you come alone anyway."

Great. Had the comment been made by anyone else, it might have caused her to change her mind about going. But she'd known Norm almost from the first day she came to work at Mercy Hospital. "Okay, I'll be there as soon as I can. I'm on foot, and it's a few blocks, so don't expect me in the next few minutes."

Joy hung up and tucked the phone into her pocket as she stepped inside the gift shop. "How has the morning been so far? Busy?" she asked Angela.

"Off and on, yes," she said.

Lacy offered her a smile. "I gave your number to Mr. Ashford. He said it was important. Other than that there haven't been any calls."

"Yes, about that." Joy bypassed the counter and stepped into the back room. She pulled her ID from her wallet and then tucked her purse into place in a drawer beside the sink. "In the future don't give it out unless I've told you to."

"Sure, okay," Lacy said. "I hope I haven't caused a problem."

"In this case, I don't think so." Joy tucked the ID into her pants pocket. "I need to run another errand. Will you two be all right a little longer?"

"Sure, we'll be fine," Angela said.

"Okay, this is not information that I want you to give to anyone except Evelyn Perry from the records department or Anne Mabry, a volunteer who would be wearing a badge with her name on it if she were to come in. Got it?"

"Sure," Angela said as Lacy nodded. "Are you going somewhere dangerous?"

"The Cathedral of St. John the Baptist," she said. "Call me if you need anything. I should be back in less than an hour."

Joy walked into the lobby then pulled out her phone and sent a text to both Anne and Evelyn. MEETING NORM AT CATHEDRAL OF ST. JOHN THE BAPTIST. DETAILS LATER.

Joy put her phone away and stepped out into the warm June day. By the time she reached the cathedral about twenty minutes later, she was more than ready to walk into the air-conditioned church.

She found Norm sitting in a pew in the back of the sanctuary. He waved her over.

"Thanks for coming," he said. "I know it seems like something out of a spy movie, but actually I'm serving lunch to the old folks in a little while, so I came here early instead of going home. I do have my reasons for not wanting to meet you at the hospital though."

"I can understand that," Joy said. "So have you thought of something else?"

"It's not that I thought of it. It's that I didn't tell you everything I knew." He let out a long breath. "I heard the thief's voice. Well, one of them anyway."

"What did it sound like? Male, female? Old, young?"

"Male. Not a kid but not old. Somewhere in between."

Joy shook her head. "Why didn't you say anything?"

"I told the cops," he said. "Look, I knew there had to be more to those trucks than just someone parking them there and leaving 'em. I figured at least one of them was stolen, you know? Thought maybe someone was dropping it there so's another one could come pick it up."

"You were thinking they were using the hospital for their rendezvous or something?"

"That's right," he said. "So I went looking around. Kept to the side of the building in the shadows. I didn't see anyone. And there wasn't anyone up front when I got to the corner."

"Was the statue there?"

He sighed. "I think so, but I can't be sure. I wasn't looking for a statue thief. I was looking for a truck thief."

"Right."

"So I went back around the same way I came, staying close to the hedge. I'd just passed the magnolia when I heard him. As I said, it was a man. The voice came out of nowhere, and it was muffled, like he was behind something. I froze in my tracks because I knew I was out there by myself."

"And yet you weren't."

"No. I sure wasn't." He pointed to his head. "The bump on my head says there was someone else there."

"Wait, what?"

Norm gestured to a spot on top of his head. "I've got a nice thick head of hair. Get that from my mother's side. Anyway, it's white, but it'll cover up a bump pretty well. You can check to see if I'm telling the truth. I don't mind."

She debated whether to take him up on it then figured she probably ought to. "Okay." Joy stood and placed her fingers on Norm's head where he indicated. Sure enough she could feel the goose egg that had risen there.

"Norm," Joy said on an exhale of breath as she sat back down, "did you get that checked out?"

He gave her an incredulous look. "It'll be fine."

"Okay, let me see if I understand. You went down the side of the building to the front and looked around the corner. You didn't see anyone, so you retraced your steps."

"Right."

"Okay, and that's when you heard the voice and got hit on the head. From behind, I'm assuming."

"Yes, from behind." He shrugged. "He caught me off guard. But I know there was no one there." He sat back in the pew. "I'm fine. It's just a bump. The buddy I play golf with was a medic in the military. He took a look at it and said it's nothing to worry about. The only thing that's truly wounded is my pride."

"Then why did you tell me?"

"You and that lady from records are investigating, so maybe what I've told you will help." He let out a long breath. "I hope you believe me. I would understand if you didn't."

"Don't worry about that," Joy said. "I think you're more reliable now that you're telling me things you didn't have to." She paused to think about what he'd told her. "I also think you're right in that the voice you heard belonged to the thief."

"But where did he come from? I know I'm not as young as I used to be, but I've never been snuck up on like that."

Joy smiled at him. "That is exactly what I hope to figure out. If you heard him again, would you recognize him?"

"I think so. At least I hope I would." He sighed. "I hope the thief is caught soon. I'm not so sure the cops will think this theft is urgent if their leads don't pan out in a few days. I'd hate to think that statue is gone for good."

Joy rose. "I've got to get back to the hospital. Thank you for trusting me with this, Norm."

She left him there in the pew and walked toward the door. Stepping back out into the sunshine, Joy retrieved her phone. ON MY WAY BACK. NORM HEARD SOMEONE. MALE VOICE. NO DESCRIPTION. DETAILS LATER.

AT THE GIFT SHOP NOW. WILL WAIT FOR YOU, Anne responded.

HEADING THERE ASAP, came Evelyn's reply.

By the time Joy stepped into the gift shop, she could hear Anne and Evelyn drinking coffee and talking to Lacy and Angela in the back room. "Sounds like I missed the party," she said as she poured coffee into her wildflower mug and joined them.

At the young women's protests, she quickly amended, "I'm teasing. You did a great job watching the store for me. Lacy, why don't you go ahead and take the rest of your shift off? And Angela, go ahead and take a fifteen-minute break. After that, would you make the rounds upstairs and see if we have any orders?"

"Thank you, Mrs. A.," Angela said as Lacy grabbed her purse and keys and raced to the door. Angela wasn't far behind.

"You didn't have to tell them that twice," Evelyn said. "Okay, they're gone. Spill the beans. What didn't Norm want to tell us this morning?"

Joy filled them in on her visit and then waited for their reactions. Anne spoke first.

"So he was embarrassed because someone got the jump on him?" She shook her head. "I'm not sure I buy that."

"It sounds fishy, Joy," Evelyn agreed.

"I wish you'd seen him, though," Joy countered. "And the bump he claimed he got? That I can confirm is real. Someone did hit him on the head." She thought for a moment and then said, "What puzzled him, and I guess me too, is how could someone sneak up on him when he'd just checked and no one was there?"

Evelyn was quiet for a moment. "I know of a way," she said. "It would explain how someone was there and then they weren't there anymore." She glanced at Anne, who nodded.

Joy was intrigued. "What?" she asked, looking from one to the other.

"Well, there are rumors," Evelyn began, "that Mercy Hospital was once a stop on the Underground Railroad. The rumors say there were a couple of secret rooms under the angel wing—the part that survived the fire. They come out near an underground tunnel that led to the harbor, where enslaved Black men, women, and children could escape to the north."

Joy felt her pulse quicken. "Really? That's amazing! But no one's found the secret rooms or the tunnel?"

Anne shook her head. "I think most people have forgotten the rumors, or sadly they just don't think it's worth looking into. I remember, years ago, there was a woman who came to Charleston and tried to get permission to conduct a search, but apparently her credentials weren't enough to satisfy the historical society."

Evelyn took a sip of her coffee. "I've been cleaning up old records and papers in the Vault as I get the time, but I haven't found anything that mentions either secret rooms or tunnels. I'm not sure I believe the rumors, but it would explain how someone could just suddenly appear behind Norm and bash him on the head."

Joy knew that Evelyn tried to spend as much time as possible organizing the archive room, which she'd christened "the Vault."

Since the records department was located in the surviving wing of the original hospital building, it was a mammoth undertaking.

Joy noticed a box next to Anne on the table. "What's that?"

Her friend's face brightened. "That's a gift I got this morning. I've been volunteering on the Alzheimer's unit recently, and there's the sweetest lady who's been there for a couple of weeks. This morning her granddaughter brought me a gift."

"That's nice," Evelyn said. "What did she bring you?"

Anne opened the box and lifted out a glass pitcher.

"Is her name Ace?" Joy asked.

"How did you know?"

"Because I met her at the art gallery. She's the woman who blew a happy thoughts bubble for Mallory."

"Small world," Anne said. "I didn't know she went by Ace. I've always called her Allison." She studied Joy. "Allison Roy, in case you were about to ask."

"Which I was. How often does Allison come to visit her grandmother?"

"Randomly, I guess. I never know when I'll see her." She paused. "Why?"

"I don't know. Just getting as much information as I can on all the moving parts that make this mystery so mysterious." Joy shrugged. "Allison's glassblowing studio is in the same building as Flavia's studio. She may know something about what you saw in the alley, Anne."

"Next time I see her, I'll talk to her about that."

"I've got some news," Joy said. "More news, I guess. I was able to get one of the roses from the statue to bloom."

"You were?" Evelyn smiled. "That's great." Then her brow furrowed. "But what does that mean for our investigation?"

"It means I've been able to replicate the rose that someone puts on the statue base. The flower that may have been left behind by the thief." She shook her head. "Or the roses and the missing statue might not be related at all. The roses started appearing well before the theft. What it doesn't do is help us to know who else figured out how to grow them."

"Let's talk about timing," Evelyn said. "What was going on the day the statue went missing?"

"It was a Tuesday night or Wednesday morning," Anne said. "Nothing exceptional happened on Tuesday on the ward where I was volunteering. And I hadn't arrived for work yet on Wednesday when it happened. I remember I walked up and found Joy at the empty base, then you walked up right after, Evelyn."

Joy let out a long breath as she went through the order of events that morning. The statue went missing. She came inside after speaking with Evelyn and Anne. Garrison Baker came in.

"Wait," Evelyn said suddenly.

"What?" Anne and Joy asked in unison.

"Angela," Evelyn said. "The Angel of Mercy disappeared and Angela Simpson arrived. She was hired despite a hiring freeze and bears a striking resemblance to the statue."

"We prayed for a miracle," Anne said. "And we've all assumed that miracle was Angela Simpson. What if it wasn't?"

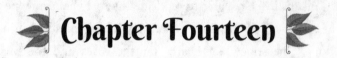

Chapter Fourteen

"I don't follow," Joy said. "I've had so many people tell me they love having Angela around. I've seen it myself. She never meets a stranger and somehow knows what people want before they do. Either she's a miracle or somebody trained that girl well."

Evelyn shrugged. "Look at the timing. What if it's not a coincidence that Angela showed up when she did?"

"But Norm said he heard a man," Anne said.

"And I believe he did," Joy said, "but I also think it took two to pull off this heist. There's no way a person could do this on his own." She put her mug on the table. "So, how do we find out about this miracle woman?"

"HR?" Anne asked.

"Good luck with that," Evelyn said. "They're not allowed to share employee records."

Joy thought of something. "We haven't ruled as inconsequential the fact that we don't know what Nancy Jones was doing between two and three that morning. She could easily have been out there too."

"If that's the case," Anne said, "why post a photo on social media? That makes no sense."

"We need to speak to her," Evelyn said. "I've tried calling her with no luck, and Shirley told me Nancy's taken a few vacation days, which seems a bit suspicious too. I'll make it my business to keep trying to contact her. She knows we're planning a shower for her, so that gives me a reason to want to meet with her."

The door opened, and Joy sighed. "I'll handle the customer and be right back." She stepped out into the shop then halted sharply.

"Hey there, Mrs. Atkins."

"Nancy," Joy managed. "How can I help you?"

Nancy shrugged. "Actually, I was coming to see if I could help you. Shirley told me everything. I guess you'd like an explanation."

She looked at a spot just past Joy's shoulder. Joy turned around to see Anne and Evelyn gaping at their guest from the doorway.

"Well, that was easier than we expected," Evelyn quipped. "Nancy, honey, we were just having coffee. Won't you join us?"

Nancy smiled as she walked past the ladies to settle at the remaining empty spot at the table. Anne put a cup of coffee in front of her. "Cream or sugar?"

"Neither," she said. "Thank you though."

"What do you know about the theft of the statue, Nancy? And why did you post that photo online?"

"Okay. First, I don't know anything about it, and I promise that's the truth. Second, I didn't post it."

"It was on your Facebook page," Anne said. "If you didn't put it there, who did?"

Nancy twisted a lock of her hair, a reluctant expression on her face. "Probably my future brother-in-law, Liam. He's a tech nerd and can do all sorts of things with computers and video games." She bit her lip and looked away. "I did pose for the picture, though. And before you ask, it wasn't on the night the statue was stolen. I did it about a week ago as a favor to Ryan, okay? Liam needed some help with a project he was working on, so I slipped out and posed for the pictures then went back up to the unit."

"So your absence from the maternity unit the other night had nothing to do with the theft of the statue?" Joy asked.

"No," Nancy said. "I promise it was just something personal I had to do."

"Ryan is your fiancé, right?" At Nancy's nod, Joy continued. "What kind of project was his brother working on?"

"A video game, I think he said. He needed some stills, some background shots."

"So he asked you to stand in front of the statue and pose, and then he digitally altered the background so that it looked like the statue—and you—were somewhere else?" Anne asked.

Nancy nodded. "Yes, I think that's what happened."

"So Liam does IT projects," Evelyn said. "Like what, besides video games?"

She shrugged. "Ryan said he has all kinds of projects for school. I promise, that's all I know." Nancy paused. "That picture looked bad. I mean, it's kind of a cool picture, but showing up when it did? That was bad."

"It was," Joy said. "Do you have anyone who will corroborate your story?"

"Liam can, of course. Ryan wasn't there that night. It was just me and Liam."

Anne looked at her. "And there won't be any problem talking to Liam, right?"

Nancy's expression told them there might be. "I'll see what I can do," she said. "He stays with Ryan when he's in town, but his project has him on the road a lot."

"Would you text me Ryan's address?" Evelyn said.

"Sure, I'll do that right now." Nancy retrieved her phone from her purse and began to type.

"Another question, then," Joy said. "Have you heard anything about how the statue disappeared? Maybe someone on the unit or another nurse in a different unit has talked about it? I mean, you were on duty that night and so were a lot of other people."

Nancy looked up at Joy, her brows furrowed. "Well," she said, "I've had lots of conversations about the statue. Everyone is talking about it. I mean, it's not every day a statue that's been in place since the early 1800s just disappears."

"Only it didn't just disappear," Anne said. "That's not possible."

"No, it's not," Nancy agreed. "So is there anything else I can help you with?"

Evelyn nodded. "Get me that guest list for the shower and send me three options for dates. I'll need that by the end of next week at the latest."

Nancy looked at her in disbelief. "So you still want to throw me a shower, even after all this?"

"Of course," Evelyn said. "Unless you don't want one."

Nancy's grin was swift and broad. "We do," she said. "And thank you so much. I'll get all of that to you well before you need it." She hurried to the door and then paused to turn around. "Thank you for believing me, ladies."

"Well, we aren't ready to say we believe you just yet," Evelyn said gently. "We'll check it all out and confirm what you've told us."

"Yes, right. I hesitate to say this, but while you're at it, you might check on Angela Simpson. She got a job here when there are no jobs to be had."

"Apparently there was a grant specifically for her position."

"And she's the only one who interviewed?" Nancy shook her head. "Still sounds fishy, but then what do I know about HR?"

She waved and then opened the door and hurried away.

"What did you think of that?" Joy asked.

"I think she's got a point," Anne told her. "It is fishy that Angela would be given a job now, of all times, and that Garrison would tell you that whoever gave that anonymous donation to fund the position did it with the requirement that Angela be hired."

"Yes, I guess so," Joy said.

"Then there's the interesting coincidence that she looks so much like the statue," Evelyn offered.

"Okay, I agree that all of these things are unusual," Joy admitted, "but do we have any reason to believe that Angela is involved in the theft of the statue? Remember, she wasn't working here when it was taken."

Anne shook her head. "I can't think of anything, but then we don't know what she did on the days leading up to the theft."

Evelyn nodded toward the door where Angela was approaching. "Now looks like as good a time as any to ask her that question."

Angela bounded into the store with her usual smile and a paper bag in her hand. "I couldn't finish my bagel, so I figured I'd drop it off here before I go upstairs."

"Angela," Joy said. "Stay a minute. We've got some questions."

"Sure," Angela said. "Is there something wrong?"

"We're just looking into some things," Joy told her. "How is it you came to be here at Mercy Hospital?"

"My understanding is there was a grant," she said.

"And you don't know who the donor was?" Anne asked.

"The lady in HR said it was anonymous. Only the administrator can know." Angela shrugged. "Why?"

"We're just curious. Did you make any trips here before the day you reported for your first day of work—other than when you interviewed, that is?"

Angela smiled. "I didn't," she said. "I looked Mercy Hospital up online and really liked what I read about it."

"That's good to hear," Evelyn said. "So tell us about yourself, Angela. Where are you from?"

"Florida," she said. "Fort Myers."

"A beach girl," Evelyn said. "So I guess you like being close to the water here."

"It's nice, but what I really like is the history. I mean, you can get lost in all the museums, historic sites, and other stuff. I heard there was a lecture at one of the colleges the other night. There was a history professor speaking, and I wanted to go. I love Charleston history." She shrugged. "But laundry prevailed."

Evelyn shifted positions. "Thank you for answering our questions. Maybe you've got questions for us. We'd love to answer them, wouldn't we?"

Angela shrugged. "No, I'm good. Anyway, I should get back to my duties. I have a feeling that Mrs. Winters in the geriatric unit is going to want her *People* magazine. I'll grab a copy, and if she doesn't want it I'll bring it back. If she does, I'll bill it to her."

"You do that," Joy said. "Once you're finished with that, you're free to go. Just come back tomorrow at the regular time."

"Thank you, Mrs. A."

"I'm glad you joined us," Anne said.

"I hope you didn't think we were too nosy," Evelyn added.

"Just curious," she said. "Not that I blame you. If Charleston's anything like Fort Myers, it's a big city, but it can feel like a small town."

"That's the truth," Anne said.

"Later, guys." Angela offered a wave, grabbed the magazine, and made her way out of the gift shop.

"Thoughts?" Joy asked when the door closed behind Angela.

"She's young and energetic," Anne said. "The staff like her, and I find her pleasant."

"Yes, she's nice," Evelyn said. "And she gets bonus points for wanting to attend a historical lecture at the college. But it's still a big coincidence that she came on the day the angel left. I just can't get past the timing of that."

Joy frowned. "But if someone was going to be planted in a hospital as an accomplice to a theft, wouldn't that happen before the theft and not after?"

"Who's to say she wasn't here before?" Evelyn asked. "We don't know that."

"She might have slipped in as a visitor at some point," Joy conceded. "But I'm just not ready to make the jump to believing that scenario yet."

Evelyn followed Angela's path to the door then stopped short. "Didn't she just tell us that she was going to take a magazine to a patient upstairs?"

"She did," Anne said as Joy nodded in agreement.

"Then why is she leaving?"

Joy and Anne hurried to see what Evelyn was looking at. Joy arrived just in time to see Angela going down the seldom-used hall that led to the parking garage. Odd. Most people used the second-floor walkway to get to the garage.

"Maybe she left something in her car she needs," Joy said.

"Hmm. Maybe," Evelyn said doubtfully. She shrugged. "Anyway, I need to get back to work. We've talked so long, I'll have to grab a sandwich from the café and work through my lunch hour."

"And Ralph's coming to take me to lunch," Anne said. "Joy, if I don't see you again before you leave, I'll see you tomorrow."

Evelyn said goodbye also, and the door closed behind them, leaving Joy alone in the gift shop. A few minutes later several customers arrived. After that, there was a steady stream for the hours around the middle of the day. Finally three o'clock arrived, and Joy put the CLOSED sign on the door and turned out the lights.

Joy had just turned onto Meeting Street when someone honked a horn behind her. She turned around to see Ralph and Anne pull over to the curb.

"Want a ride?" Anne called.

Joy slipped into the back seat. "Did you two have a nice lunch?"

Ralph Mabry, a friendly man with styled gray hair and kind eyes that seemed to miss nothing, smiled at her in the rearview mirror. "We got takeout and found a nice quiet bench at Joe Riley Park," he said.

"Oh, is that the one with the pineapple fountain?" Joy asked. "I keep meaning to get there. I've heard the whole park is just beautiful."

Anne turned in her seat. "It really is. We sat underneath one of the pavilions overlooking the harbor. With the gorgeous breeze coming off the water, you'd never know it was June in South Carolina."

"I'm glad you two could get away to do that," Joy said, smiling at her.

Anne looked at Ralph then again at Joy. "We did see something interesting on our way to the park," she said.

"What was that?" Joy asked.

"Well, you remember it looked like Angela was going to the parking garage earlier?"

"Yes," said Joy.

"Ralph picked me up, and on our way to the park we saw Anne going into the historical society. Now why would she tell us she was going to see a patient and then not do it?"

Joy sat back and let out a long breath as she thought over the possibilities. Finally she spoke up. "What would make her lie to us?"

"I don't know," Anne said.

"Ladies," Ralph said, "I want to caution you about this adventure you're on right now."

His use of the word *adventure* made Joy think of Mallory and the games she played with the little girl. But this was no game. Although it might be argued that it very much had become an adventure.

"Ralph," Anne said gently. "We are taking every precaution. I've told you that."

"You have, and I appreciate that. I also appreciate the spirit in which your help is being offered. You said that Garrison Baker could lose his job over all this. He's a good man, and that would be a shame."

"It would," Joy said. "And then there's the statue. She needs to be back where she belongs."

"Right." He glanced at Joy again in the rearview mirror. "I want those things too. But I don't want them at the expense of my wife or her friends' safety, and I don't want you all doing anything without the permission of the proper authorities."

"Nor do I," Joy agreed.

He nodded. "Okay. I see we are of the same mind."

"I told you," Anne said.

A few minutes later, Joy stepped out onto her driveway. "Thanks for the lift," she called as they drove away.

Joy had barely set her purse and keys on the kitchen counter when her phone rang. It was Anne.

"Did you forget something?"

"Listen, Joy," Anne said. "There's a man watching your house."

"A man?" She shook her head and walked toward the front of the house. Because the home sat so close to the street, she never opened her curtains unless she was home. Today was no exception.

Joy peered out the peephole of her door, her phone still at her ear. "I don't see anyone."

"There was a man out there. A big guy with short hair and a beard." She could hear Ralph say something. "Ralph says the fellow looked like a linebacker."

Joy went to the window and moved her curtain just enough to get a better view of the street. There. She saw him.

"I'm going to put you on speaker," she said.

"Joy? What are you about to do?"

"Shh …" Joy said as she opened the door. "Colin," she called to the man loitering across the street. "Colin Guest. Were you waiting for me to get home?"

"Are you all right?" Anne asked. "Do you know the guy?"

"Yes," Joy said as Colin crossed Mercy Street and came toward her house. "It's Claudia Guest's nephew. I'm perfectly safe. I met him at the studio the other night and asked him to contact me if he had more information."

"You gave a practical stranger your address?" Anne asked.

"No, I didn't, but his aunt is my neighbor, and I did tell him that I bought a house on Mercy Street. Finding me wouldn't have been difficult."

"Joy, be careful."

"Don't be silly. We'll talk later." She hung up the phone and tucked it into her pocket.

Colin wore a sheepish look as he stopped beside her. "I've been thinking about our conversation at the studio. Have you thought about what I said?"

"I have," she told him. "But I'm confused. I don't understand what you meant when you told me that it isn't about the statue. What isn't about the statue? The theft? Something else?"

"Okay, so I wasn't sure what I was going to do with this, but showing you is the right thing. I was over at my aunt's house for Sunday dinner. She's big on that. I was sitting beside her at the table while she was scrolling through her phone." He paused to turn his back to the street as a car drove past. "Anyway, when I saw it, I couldn't believe she had that."

"Colin," Joy said, "I have no idea what you're talking about. What did she have?"

"Yeah, I know. I'm rambling. I mean, I knew my aunt was capable of things that, well ... shoot." He snatched his phone out of his pocket. "I'll just show you."

"Yes, all right," Joy said.

"Here it is. She left her phone on the kitchen counter when she went to the bathroom, and I sent the picture she had to my phone."

Colin thrust the phone in her direction. Joy looked down but there was a glare on the screen. "I'm sorry, I can't see anything."

He moved closer to her house, bringing them both into the shade. "Here," he said, "try now."

Joy looked down at the phone, and her heart thudded against her chest. There, in Colin's outstretched hand, was a photograph of a cream-colored Noisette rosebud with the slightest sign of a crimson center.

"This looks very much like ..." She swallowed the words, unwilling to admit the flower looked like the one locked away in her garage. "Like the Noisette we discussed at the garden club on Saturday." She met Colin's steady gaze. "The one she told me was impossible to propagate."

"Yeah, I heard all about that meeting."

"From your aunt?"

He colored slightly. "No, I uh, had a friend there." Colin shook his head. "Anyway, I don't think you get what's happening here."

"Sure I do," Joy said. "Your aunt has propagated a rose that she said doesn't exist." She froze. *A rose that someone has been leaving on the Angel of Mercy statue for months* went unsaid.

"No, ma'am," he said. "That isn't my aunt's rose. That's yours."

Chapter Fifteen

JOY FROWNED AT COLIN GUEST. "No, it can't be my rose. Mine is …"

Her heart thudded again. She stared at the picture. Sure enough, the grow light above the bloom was the same one Rob had put up for her. And the bright yellow wooden surface beneath was unmistakably the workbench that was now home to her seedlings.

"How did your aunt get a picture of my rose?" Joy managed. "And how did you know it's mine and not hers?"

Colin's phone vibrated, and he looked at the screen. "Look, I gotta go. My sister just had a baby, and her husband is deployed, so she needs me to make a run for diapers for her. I'm not going to answer that question or any others you might have. I know what I've heard and what I see here. That's your flower, and my aunt has a picture of it on her phone. Now do with that what you will."

"Why are you telling me this?" she asked him.

"Because I don't like the way she'll do whatever she can to get her way."

Joy looked past Colin and saw the Mabrys' sedan turning the corner up ahead. Colin must have seen her eyes widen, because he looked over his shoulder and then sprinted away.

"Her way in what?" she called but Colin had already moved too far away to respond.

Ralph pulled his car to the curb, and Anne spilled out first. "What happened?" she said as she looked down the street at Colin's retreating back.

"Did he threaten you?" Ralph demanded.

"Come inside, and I'll tell you about it." She opened the door and let them in, then closed the door and locked it. "But first I'd like you to come with me out to the garage. I need to check on the roses."

She found the lock still in place and the rose cuttings exactly where she'd left them. Even the one that bloomed with the impossible crimson center was still right where she'd left it.

With no windows to look through and a locked door barring entrance, how did Claudia manage to get that photograph? Joy took a calming breath as another possibility came to her.

"Maybe it wasn't Claudia?"

"What's that?" Anne asked.

Joy turned around to face her friends. "Colin showed me a photograph of my rose." She pointed to the new bloom. "The rose I'm growing from one of the Noisettes that were left on the statue."

Ralph's normally calm expression flashed anger. "You're saying he broke in here and took pictures of it?"

"Just the one that I know about," she said. "He all but told me Claudia did it." She shook her head. "Come into the kitchen, and I'll make coffee."

"None for me," Ralph said. "But thank you."

"Same," Anne agreed. "However, an iced tea sounds fabulous."

"Fabulous," Joy echoed. "That's Mallory's new favorite word, thanks to Flavia Bowe."

They walked into the kitchen, and Joy retrieved two glasses from the cupboard.

"Make that three," Ralph said. "Do you mind if I check things out in your house? I know you said it was just your garage that was photographed, but if they got in there and locked up again, anything is possible."

"I'd appreciate that," Joy told him.

Anne sat down at the small round table in the breakfast area and watched as Joy filled the glasses with ice then reached for the tea. Finally, she spoke. "Do you trust him?"

"Colin?" At Anne's nod, Joy shrugged. "Right now, I don't know. He seemed genuinely upset about Claudia having the photograph on her phone. In fact, the topic of his aunt didn't bring out the best in him when we spoke at the studio either. The thought has occurred to me that he's not telling me the truth, and that may very well be the case. Not to mention that he wouldn't tell me how he knew from the photograph that the rose was mine. As far as I know he's never seen the inside of my garage."

Joy placed a glass of tea in front of Anne and another at the place next to her for Ralph. Then she went back for her own and took the glass back to the table to sit across from Anne.

"You always make the best sweet tea," Anne said.

"The secret's in the sugar. Add it right after you take out the teabags. Give it a few minutes to melt and then add the cold water." She shrugged. "That's how my mama taught me."

Anne smiled. "Now all I have to do is remember that."

"Everything looks fine," Ralph announced as he returned to the kitchen. "All doors and windows are locked."

"Thank you, Ralph," Joy said.

He settled beside his wife and squeezed her hand before taking up his tea glass. "Now that we've got the lay of the land, Joy, what are you going to do about what you know?"

She sighed. "That's what I'm trying to decide. I think the only things that are in danger of disappearing are the seedlings, so I can't leave them out there."

"We can take them with us," he said. "No one would think to look at our place."

"I appreciate that, Ralph, but they require a lot of care. I'm the only one of us who knows how to keep them alive."

"She has a point," Anne told him. "Although I would try."

"No, I think I need to move them into the house for now. I can get Rob to see if the grow light can be reinstalled somewhere else."

"I can do that," Ralph announced. "Where do you want it to go?"

"Good question."

After some debate, they settled on a relocation to the guest bathroom upstairs. Ralph easily removed the light from its place in the garage and hung it by its chains from the shower curtain rod. With a tarp normally used for painting lining the tub and several pieces of plywood over the top of it, the three of them managed to set up a makeshift greenhouse.

"My work here is done," Ralph said with a chuckle. "I've made many home visits during my time as a pastor, but I've never been called on to relocate roses to a bathtub."

"There's a first time for everything," Joy said, laughing. "Do y'all want more tea?"

Ralph looked at his watch. "We ought to be getting home, don't you think, Annie? The sitter will be wondering where we've gone."

"Yes, of course," Anne said. She turned to leave the room then whipped back around. "Oh Joy," she said, "I didn't get a chance to tell you, but I asked a few questions about that man who was in the surgery unit. Alan Parker? One of the nurses said she overhead some suspicious talk while he was under her care. Phone calls that sounded like he was making plans to pull off something big."

"Was she specific about the plans?"

"No," Anne said, "but she was sure that he was using his time at Mercy to work on something he had going on. She couldn't say why she felt it was suspicious other than he seemed to be talking in code. Saying things that didn't make sense to her."

"Well, maybe he just didn't want to have a stranger know what he was saying. That doesn't automatically make what he's saying suspect," Joy said.

"Agreed." Anne shrugged. "But she also told me that the type of operation he had is generally day surgery."

"But he stayed a week, didn't he?"

Anne nodded. "I asked if maybe there were complications that kept him there. This is where it gets interesting. She told me that after the first two days, he treated his visit like he was at a hotel. He was staying because he wanted to stay there." She pondered that thought. An arrangement like that would have required special allowances from someone in authority. "The nurses figured he was hiding out there. But that's just conjecture."

Ralph frowned. "Conjecture is hardly facts, honey."

"You're right, I know. And we certainly can't go looking into Alan Parker's medical records. But most people can't wait to get out of the hospital, so it seems odd that someone would pay extra to stay there."

"I'll put that in my notes," Joy said.

Ralph held out his hands. "Now how about I pray for you and for your safety before we go?"

"I would love that." Joy grasped her friends' hands and closed her eyes.

At the prayer's conclusion, Joy bid Anne and Ralph goodbye and then locked the doors behind them. With her seedlings safe inside the house, she felt a little less anxious about the events of the day.

She made a sandwich and thawed out some soup she had left over and frozen last week. She was still trying to get a handle on cooking for one. She carried her soup and sandwich to the table and gathered her suspect list and other notes to go over as she ate.

She stalled as she reached Garrison Baker's name on her list. Had he authorized a criminal to remain under the hospital's roof just because he was paying for the privilege?

She thought once again about the budget dilemma. What would Garrison do to make ends meet?

Joy took her dishes to the sink and washed them, thinking about what a long day it had been. It seemed like eons since she'd seen Garrison that morning. She decided some well-earned dessert was in order, and she knew just what she wanted. Soup wasn't the only thing in her freezer. It was just a matter of seconds before she had two chocolate chip cookies in the microwave with a marshmallow sandwiched between them. Wilson's favorite—and pretty much nightly—snack was his own invention, or so he claimed.

Just as she was finishing the last bite and licking the s'morey goodness off her fingers, the email alert dinged on her phone. She rinsed and dried her hands, swiped the screen, and saw Leah Ainsworth's name.

Enjoyed our meeting. I wonder what you know about Brown Construction. Odd question, I know, but I'm hoping you've got an answer.

Joy frowned. It was odd. She'd asked Leah about the statue and nothing else. How could Leah have known that Joy was familiar with Brown Construction? Joy was certain she hadn't mentioned it.

Then she thought of Flavia. Of course. They worked in the same space, and Flavia's brother was Joy's architect. So Flavia would know that Joy used Brown Construction as her builder.

Joy quickly typed out a message to Leah, telling her how much she loved the work done by Brown Construction with Richard's supervision. She added her cell number in case Leah had any more questions.

Her phone dinged with a text from Evelyn. Mind a quick call?

Joy texted back, Not at all! A few seconds later her phone rang. "Hi, Joy," Evelyn said. "I compared the ancestry site results to the copy of Claudia Guest's family tree that I was able to get from the historical society. There's a significant difference between the two. On the ancestry site there's this extra branch that isn't on the one I found at the historical society. I can't figure out where it goes. From what we could see—I asked James to look too—Claudia's great-great-grandmother has one more daughter on the ancestry site than she does in the historical society records. There's a date of birth and a birth certificate but nothing else. As I said, the historical society doesn't make note of her at all. Oh, and I made some discreet inquiries. No one admitted to having a meeting with Angela Simpson."

"Interesting."

"We'll keep digging. I don't know if it means something, but it is curious."

Joy agreed, and the pair chatted for a few more minutes before bidding each other goodbye. After hanging up, Joy went to check on her indoor rose garden before calling it a night.

As she lay in her bed trying to fall asleep, her mind churned over the information she'd noted this evening. Then her mind turned to what Evelyn and Anne had told her about rumors of secret rooms and tunnels.

Thus far, Evelyn's search of old records had turned up nothing. She'd admitted there was still much to sort through, but her job did keep her busy—when Joy wasn't pulling her away to chase leads.

It could take months before something like that turned up. If only there was an old blueprint of the hospital somewhere …

Joy sat straight up in bed, her heart pounding. There were maps and photographs of the hospital on Garrison's office walls. Some were new while others were obviously very old. There had to be close to a hundred pieces jammed together on those walls.

Could one of them possibly have a diagram of the location of the tunnels? There was only one way to find out.

Chapter Sixteen

JOY STEPPED OFF THE ELEVATOR and onto the plush carpet of the administration level of the hospital. Bypassing the bench where she'd waited for Garrison last time, she walked straight down the hall toward his office.

As before, no one else had arrived yet. Most of the people who worked in administration wouldn't be here until nine o'clock, and it was not yet six thirty. She'd awakened extra early, if it was possible to awake from a night where it felt as if she'd never actually fallen asleep.

The morning was rainy, likely from the tropical storm still churning toward them, so Joy had driven today. No light shone under Garrison's door, but she knocked anyway.

"Come in."

Letting out a long breath, she opened the door and found Mercy Hospital's administrator at his desk with only a small banker's lamp illuminating a stack of papers. Beside the papers was a notepad. The rest of the room was in shadows with only the pale orange light of the coming dawn seeping through the purple gloom.

"Good morning, Joy," he said, though his voice and his countenance told her he was anything but cheerful.

"Good morning, Garrison. Am I interrupting something?"

Garrison replaced the cap on his pen and set it aside then leaned away from the desk to stretch his back. "Would you mind hitting that light switch next to you, please?"

Joy did as he asked, and the room blazed with overhead illumination. Garrison blinked to adjust his eyes to the change in light. Then he rubbed them with his fists. Finally, he returned his attention to her.

"Sorry, I wasn't expecting visitors this early. How can I help you?"

She took a step toward the door. "I can come back."

"No, it's fine." He shrugged. "I wasn't getting anywhere anyway."

"Okay, well, I didn't actually come to see you."

Garrison's brows rose. "No?"

She shook her head. "I wondered if maybe I could look at your maps." She pointed to the wall to her right.

"Sure. Go ahead," he said with a sweep of his hand. "Is there something in particular you're looking for?"

"Something old," she said. "The 1860s maybe. I'm more interested in blueprints or maps than photographs."

"Well," he said, exhaustion seeping into his tone, "go ahead. To be honest, I have no idea what's on the walls other than it's nice to look at them from over here at the desk I'm chained to. It's been a long few months, Joy."

"I'm sorry," she said. "You inherited a mess."

He shrugged. "Henry was a mentor. Like a father to me. And I know he did his best. But the board had him hamstrung because he wouldn't go along with them on certain things. That's what I've inherited. I'm not planning to go along with them either. So here I am, trying to figure it all out."

"I'll pray that you do," she said, aware that she might be speaking to the man who'd stolen the statue to do exactly what he'd just said. To figure it out.

"And if you don't mind, I'm going to take a walk and see if I can get my brain to work again."

"My coffeepot is set to come on at six forty-five, but you can always go down and turn it to manual. It brews pretty quickly."

"I just may do that."

He offered a smile and walked out, leaving Joy to her search. But seconds later she thought of something. She followed Garrison down the corridor and called to him just as he was about to get into the elevator.

"Do you mind answering a quick theoretical question?"

He cast a reluctant glance at the elevator then allowed the doors to close without stepping inside. "Okay, what's that?"

"If someone wanted to stay in the hospital longer than they were supposed to, say a patient has had an operation that requires a short stay—overnight, I'll say—but that patient doesn't want to go home yet, can he stay as long as he wants? Or she?" Joy hastily added.

"You mean would we allow a patient to dictate the length of his stay?" He paused. "Or hers?" he added with a sly grin.

"Yes, that's right."

"Absolutely not. Patients are admitted at the doctor's discretion and discharged under the same protocol."

"With no exceptions?"

"Exactly. If the doctor says stay, the patient stays unless they choose to leave without a doctor's approval. But if the doctor says go, that's that. Does that help?"

"Thank you, Garrison. Yes, it does."

He pushed the button, and the elevator doors opened again. "Close my office door behind you when you leave, please."

Then he was gone. Joy wondered if she should bring it to his attention that apparently a patient had been able to persuade a doctor somewhere to break protocol. It had probably cost Alan Parker a pretty penny.

She walked back into the office and went to the wall where most of the old maps were hung. Each gold-framed piece bore a nameplate with a date. She moved quickly to what appeared to be a blueprint. The date proclaimed this to be 1843.

Squinting to see the details, Joy quickly determined there was nothing unusual about this drawing. She moved to another one, and then another. With each subsequent drawing, the hospital's changes through the years were shown.

Joy had almost given up when she spied a small hand drawing on brown paper. Unlike the others, this ornate frame bore no plate identifying the year. She had to kneel to look closer.

The words MERCY HOSPITAL had been written across the top in block letters with ink that was fading. Beneath that in smaller script, the author of the drawing had written just one word: ADDITIONALS.

"Additionals?"

She shook her head. This one looked like the others except that in places there were dashed lines. It could be something as simple as running lines to fuel gas lighting or as interesting as noting a secret room.

Joy snapped a picture with her phone and continued her search. Two more frames indicated they contained items from the 1860s and 1870s, so she took photographs of those as well.

Maybe with some study, once the pictures were enlarged, rooms—or even passages or tunnels—might reveal themselves. Also, Evelyn might be able to use the data on this drawing to find other related historical information.

She stood and stepped back from the wall, satisfied that if there was anything helpful there, she had found it. She left the office, closed the door behind her, and walked to the elevator. As she waited, she texted Anne and Evelyn to tell them about her find and attached the pictures she'd taken of the hospital plans.

When the elevator door opened, Joy looked up to see Shirley leaning against the back wall. "Good morning," Joy said to her. "How are you?"

"I'm good," Shirley said with a smile. "How are you?"

Joy put her phone in her pocket as she stepped into the elevator. "I'm good too. Where are you headed?" She looked at the bank of numbers. None of them were lit, which probably meant Shirley wanted to get off at this level. She stepped to the side to make room for her to pass.

Instead, Shirley reached over, inserted a key into the "authorized personnel only" lock, and then punched the helipad button. "I could tell you, but it'd be a lot better to show you."

It took just a few seconds to reach the top, where Shirley led Joy off the elevator and through two sets of double doors that opened to the rooftop. They stood in the center of the massive area, and Joy caught her breath as she faced east and looked out over Charleston

Harbor. Brilliant oranges, pinks, purples, and yellows streaked the sky and were reflected in the mirrored surface of the water. The strong salty breeze blew her hair back from her face, and she felt her mind as well as her body relaxing and just taking it all in.

"God sure knows how to put on a show, doesn't He?" Shirley said. "Every time I come up here, I'm reminded that He can handle things in my life just fine, thank you very much."

Joy breathed a prayer of thanksgiving and praise and then said, "I'm so glad you brought me up here. Thank you, Shirley."

Shirley turned toward the doors. "I would love to stay longer, but my shift isn't over yet. I'm only taking a quick break. But Joy, you can text me and we can arrange to come back up here sometime—I try to see a sunrise two or three times a week—whenever I can take a quick break."

"I would love to come again," Joy said as they made their way to the elevator. "How is your mama doing these days, by the way?"

"She's keeping everyone at the senior center on their toes," Shirley said. "But she does have her moments." She chuckled. "About two weeks ago we went to the eye doctor to get her glasses adjusted. She'd dropped them and bent the frame. It only took a few minutes to do. Since then, Mama's been insisting that the woman who adjusted them gave her back the wrong pair—she keeps saying 'these aren't my glasses.'"

Joy was puzzled. "But when they adjust your glasses, they don't take them anywhere."

Shirley rolled her eyes. "Try telling Mama that. So yesterday, she took her glasses off to clean them, and all of a sudden she holds them up and says, 'See? Right here, it says "Made in China." These glasses were made in China. I've never been to China in my life—I told you they weren't mine!'"

Joy was still smiling when she got off the elevator on the ground floor and walked to the gift shop. Anne was waiting for her. "I couldn't sleep," Anne said with a wave of her hand. "That incident with the rose had my mind reeling."

"Mine too." Joy unlocked the door and held it open. "Let's get some coffee."

Anne yawned. "I wouldn't turn it down."

Before Joy entered the shop, she saw Evelyn and Nancy coming down the hallway together. "I think the morning just got more interesting," she said to Anne. "Hi Nancy, Evelyn," she called. "Do you ladies have a minute?"

Nancy smiled. "I sure do. Evelyn and I were talking about available dates for the shower. You guys are super sweet for doing this for Ryan and me."

"We can talk about that," Joy said, "but I wanted to talk about something else first, if you don't mind."

Nancy followed Evelyn and Joy into the shop. "I don't mind at all."

Anne had already busied herself getting four mugs of coffee poured. She put the creamer and sugar packets on the table as the others sat down.

Joy reached for her mug. "I just wanted to ask you if you've heard anything about the statue since we last talked about it."

Nancy took a sip of coffee. "I have, as a matter of fact. Ryan told me that Liam guessed that it might be a college prank. You know, a fraternity dare or something."

"Did they say anything more than that?"

"You'd have to ask them," she told Joy. "I'm not really into all that. I mean, I wish the statue wasn't gone, but I park in the back, so I never really saw her anyway."

"Would you mind if I contacted Ryan or Liam about what they know?" Joy asked.

Nancy shrugged. "Not at all. I'll text you Ryan's contact info. Like I said, Liam stays with him while he's in town for the summer, so if he happens to be with Ryan when you call, you can talk to both of them."

"Thank you, Nancy," Joy said. "I appreciate you keeping your ears open when you're on your shift too."

They shifted their discussion to the wedding shower and finally settled on a date that was convenient for all of them. Evelyn drained the last of her coffee and stood. "I'll be sending out the invitations to staff next week so if you've got any additions or changes to the guest list and date, let me know today."

"It's perfect just the way it is," Nancy said. "I know I keep saying it, but thank you, ladies." She looked at her watch. "Oh boy, I need to get moving." She waved goodbye and rushed away.

A couple of minutes later as the three friends were cleaning up, all three of their phones dinged at the same time.

Evelyn looked at her phone and chuckled. "Nancy must've had a moment on the elevator to send Ryan's info."

"You know," Joy said after reading the address on the contact she'd just received, "I've got Lacy covering for me this morning. I think I'll pay Ryan a visit."

"I wish I could go with you," Evelyn said. "But I'm slammed this morning. Plus I had hoped to try to cross-reference the drawings you sent against our records."

Anne gave her a regretful look. "And I'm needed to assist with patients today. With that tropical storm heading our way, the hospital has asked for an assessment of all inpatient cases to see who can be discharged and who absolutely has to stay. That's going to give the nurses extra work, which means the volunteers will need to pick up the slack."

"What's all the fuss with this tropical storm?" Joy asked. "When I lived in Houston, we didn't pay much attention to those things unless they were bearing down on us."

"Considering this one is supposed to make landfall over the weekend..." Evelyn shook her head. "I guess the *Night at the Museum* event will be canceled."

"Of course it will. The storm should have increased to hurricane strength by then," Anne said. "What do you think of her being named Hurricane Joy?"

"I'm ignoring that just like I'm ignoring the storm altogether right now. I'm more worried about finding that statue."

Anne and Evelyn left to start their mornings, and a few minutes later the gift shop door opened and Angela came in. "Good morning, Mrs. A. I know I'm not supposed to come in until this afternoon, but I promised Mrs. Winters I would read her magazine to her this morning."

"That's fine, Angela," Joy said. "But I need to ask you a question. Yesterday you said you were going to take a magazine to a patient, but instead you went to the historical society. Now, what you were doing there isn't any of my business, but I need to know that you're not neglecting the patients."

Silence fell between them as Angela fidgeted with the shoulder strap of her tote bag. Finally she met Joy's gaze. "You're right, I was there, but I promise, I didn't neglect my patients. I did come back and visit Mrs. Winters." She turned. "Do you mind if I go to her now? She has PT in half an hour."

Joy waved to her with a troubled heart. How could she work with someone she couldn't trust? She busied herself with inventory until Lacy showed up for her shift at nine. Joy gave instructions for the morning to her and then headed to her car.

Joy added the contact information she'd received from Nancy into her GPS and drove the short distance to the address. Ryan Sterling's home was a condo not far from the naval base. There were two cars outside. Joy walked past them and knocked on the door.

A bleary-eyed bearded young man in black sweatpants and a plain blue T-shirt opened the door. He didn't look like someone Nancy would marry, but who was Joy to judge?

"Do you know what time it is?" he asked as he ran a hand through thick blond hair.

"Ryan Sterling?"

"Negative," he said.

"Is he here?" she asked.

"Lady, do you know what time it is?"

"Could I speak with him?" she asked. "It's important."

The door closed. Just when Joy thought she wouldn't get any further response, the door opened again. This man resembled the other but was taller, clean-shaven, and more rested. He looked as if he might be on his way to the office.

"Ryan Sterling?"

He nodded.

"I'm Joy Atkins, a friend of Nancy's. I won't take but a minute. She told us about the angel statue possibly being stolen as a prank. I'm working on an investigation, and we're trying to get it back."

Ryan leaned against the door. "It was just a rumor. It was confirmed in yesterday's alumni newsletter. Would you like to see it?"

"Please," she said.

He left for a moment and then returned with what looked like a newspaper. "Right there," he said after folding back the pages to reveal a full-page article on the theft of the angel. "See. The fraternities all denied it, and the police have cleared them."

Joy skimmed the article then nodded. "Okay. Thank you for your time."

Ryan shrugged. "The hospital has been good to Nancy. She said some ladies are even giving us a wedding shower. Well, her a shower, although she's marrying me, so I guess technically that makes it us."

"I know," Joy said. "I'm one of them."

"Are you gift shop, records, or volunteer? That's how she describes you."

"Gift shop," Joy said.

He reached out to shake her hand. "Well, Joy, I appreciate that. You ladies have really treated my fiancée well. We owe you." Then his face went sober. "You really want that statue back, don't you?"

"I do," she said. "And so do a lot of people."

Ryan seemed to be considering what he would say next. Then he glanced over his shoulder. "Liam, put some shoes on."

Joy could hear grumbling from behind the door.

"Just do it."

A few minutes later the same disheveled man reappeared at the door beside Ryan. "This is my brother Liam. He designs video games. He's here working on a top-secret game."

"That's impressive," Joy said, unable to imagine what would make a video game top secret.

"Tell her what it's about," Ryan said.

Liam grumbled.

"Dude, you're living here for free until the wedding. This lady is a friend of Nancy's. Tell her what your game is about."

"It's a risk," Liam said. "Ideas get stolen by very unlikely people."

"Your secret is safe with me," Joy said.

"It's just a game. It isn't real life," Liam said.

Joy nodded but otherwise remained silent.

"It's part of a series of games that a company in New York is planning to launch next year. They recruited me at NYU and had me sign a nondisclosure."

"I assure you I won't be repeating this to anyone but the two women who are investigating with me." She shifted her attention to Ryan. "That would be records and volunteer."

"Yeah, Liam," Ryan said. "I'll vouch for all three."

"Okay, each game is set in a city. I was assigned Charleston, since I grew up here."

"These games have plots or quests or something like that, right?" Joy asked. "What's yours?"

"I guess you could say I ripped it from the headlines. I'd already decided to use the hospital because of its cool history and also because it's so close to Charleston Harbor. I got here a couple of weeks ago and did some filming. Then, when the statue was taken, I decided that'd make a great plot for the game. Then they predicted a hurricane. How cool is that? So the quest is the search to find the missing angel before a hurricane hits Charleston and wipes out everything."

Chapter Seventeen

"Oh," Joy said on an exhale of breath.

"Yeah," Ryan added.

"I had to do a ton of research," Liam said. "I knew a lot about the city, but I didn't really know about Mercy Hospital. When I decided to use it for my game world, I figured I best get on it, ya know? Finding out more about the place, I mean. So I did."

"What did you find out?" Joy managed, the shock still settling around her.

"Lots of things," he said. "Like, it's super old. And most of it was burned down during the Civil War. The part of the building that was close to the statue was the only part that was still standing. Like the statue protected it."

"Right," Joy said. "That's part of Mercy Hospital's history. So you planned the game around taking the statue. So maybe you really did take it?"

"Lady, that's crazy. Why on earth would I do that?"

She shook her head. "That's what I'm trying to find out."

"Well, you can cross me off whatever list you've got going in your head. I'm just filming. I'm not stealing."

"Could I see what you've been recording?" At his reluctant expression, she said, "It's only to see if it will help in locating the statue. I assure you I'm not interested in creating a video game to compete with yours."

Liam stepped back to allow her to enter. "Come on in."

Joy followed him through a living area filled with a massive leather sofa in one corner and the biggest television she'd ever seen in the other. The dining area was adjacent to the kitchen in the back of the condo.

There on a table was a wearable video camera attached by a cord to a laptop computer. Liam opened the laptop and clicked the mouse a few times.

"Here's the file of videos," Liam said. "You can go ahead and watch these if you want. The last one, the long one, I filmed the night the statue went missing, but when I left the hospital, it was still there. I promise you."

He walked into the living area and left her to choose which of the three videos she wanted to see first. Since there were dates but no labels, she clicked on the first one and watched as the file opened.

Immediately, exterior footage of the hospital in bright sunshine came up on the screen. As the camera panned across the front of Mercy Hospital, the statue came into view. Then the image darkened to black.

Next came the same image—the hospital's front exterior—as the sun set. The bricks shimmered orange then slowly faded.

Liam came back into the dining room. "Do you want me to send them to you so you don't have to watch them here?"

"That would be great." She stood and allowed Liam to sit in front of the computer.

"What's your email address?"

She told him and watched while he sent the three videos to her. When he was done, he looked up at Joy. "Check your phone to be sure you got 'em," he said.

Joy looked and then nodded. "Thank you, Liam. I won't take up more of your time. You've been very helpful. If you think of anything else that might give us any clues as to what has happened to the statue, please let me know."

"I will," he said. "I just wish it wasn't really gone."

"Me too." Joy tucked her phone into her purse and returned to her car. Though she wanted to watch all three videos right now, her responsibilities at the gift shop couldn't be ignored.

But later that afternoon, the minute she got home from work, Joy went straight to her computer to download the videos. Her phone rang as she watched the bar scroll across the screen. She snatched it up without looking to see who was calling.

Of course it would be Anne or Evelyn, wanting to know what was on the videos.

"Hello, Joy, it's Richard Bowe."

She startled at the unexpected sound of a man's voice. "Richard? How are you?"

"I'm great, despite the fact that it appears my big performance at *Night at the Museum* will be canceled. I know that's the nature of trying to plan things during hurricane season, but honestly, I'm disappointed."

"Oh, that's too bad."

"Anyway, that isn't why I called. Since I'm unexpectedly free of all rehearsals this week, I wondered if you'd like me to come in and check on the items left on your punch list. I understand Brown Construction hasn't followed up on that."

"I, well…" She thought of the rose garden blooming in her upstairs bath. "You know what, Richard, I really don't want them working unsupervised. So it would either have to be on Saturday or a weekday after three thirty."

Richard was silent so long that she thought the call might have dropped.

"Right, okay," he said. "Another alternative is that I can come and watch whoever Leticia sends out. She's in charge now. Has been for almost a year. India is far too busy with her book tours to do anything related to the business. It's a shame it was left to her. Harold should have known his wife had no head for being in charge of anything other than telling ladies how to grow plants."

Not knowing how to respond to that, Joy said, "If you were here during the work, then they could do it at your convenience."

"Well, I guess I'll see what I can arrange. Might as well get this handled."

"Right. Let me know when you've got new information on the time." She thought of something. "Richard, you're a Civil War reenactor, right?"

"Guilty as charged," he said with a chuckle. "Why?"

"I've been learning more about the Angel of Mercy statue, and it's fascinating how it goes so far back in local history."

"Just how far depends on who's telling the story," he said. "Was there something specific you were wondering about?"

"A few things, actually. Which side of the Butler or Ford debate do you think is correct?"

He laughed again. "You go right to the hard question, don't you?"

"It's the question I'm most curious about," she said.

"As a historian, I rely on accurate historical research. If there's a paper trail or, failing that, some other infallible evidence, then I call it fact. In this case, there's very little of that. The Butler family claims they paid to have the statue sculpted, and the Fords say the same thing. Apparently even when the statue was new, the debate was raging."

"Why?"

"Pride, Joy." He paused. "The story that's been handed down by people unrelated to the Butlers and Fords is that both have taken credit for that statue ever since the beginning."

"What about the sculptor? Wouldn't he know?"

"That's an excellent question. No one knows who sculpted the piece. I suppose if we knew that, we might be able to track the records through him."

"Interesting," she said. "Don't artists usually sign their work?"

"I would say so." Richard was quiet a moment. "Though I've never seen a signature on her. Have you?"

"No, but I haven't looked either."

"Nor have I."

"Maybe when she's returned, we'll get a chance to search for one."

"I do hope she is returned," Richard said. "And maybe we'll find out that the sculptor not only signed it but also wrote 'to the Fords' or 'to the Butlers with my greatest esteem.' Wouldn't that be great?"

It was Joy's turn to laugh. "That certainly would make the answer to the debate much simpler, wouldn't it?"

"It would indeed. Now, back to your punch list. I'll talk to Leticia and find out when I can arrange to meet the workers there. Then I'll clear the time with you."

"That sounds fine. Thank you, Richard."

She hung up and returned her attention to the videos. As she'd done earlier, she chose the first one and clicked on it to start. It was obvious that Liam was shooting exteriors only on this file. In each segment, the filming was done in the daylight and then again in the same locations at night.

Joy closed out the file and opened the next one. The scenes were similar. Nothing of note beyond the fact that the moon shone full and high in the night sky in the second one. She closed that one and moved her cursor to the third one. Unlike the previous two, which were between three and four minutes, this one was about fifteen minutes long.

This time the clip opened with Liam's face. As he'd said, the footage was shot at night, and Liam was holding the camera up to himself. He appeared to be crouched in shrubbery somewhere. Then he turned around, and the camera wobbled, causing the image to go out of focus.

When the movement stopped and the focus returned, an image of the statue showed on the screen.

"I'm trying something different on this one," Liam said into the camera, his image ghostly in the low light. "The exteriors are done, but I need more footage of the statue."

The picture whirled and wobbled as Liam turned the camera to face away from himself. After a few seconds of what seemed to be an earthquake, it steadied, and Liam stepped into the frame again and appeared to adjust the angle of the lens. He grinned. "I've jammed it into the hedge so I don't have to hold it steady."

Joy saw Liam walking toward the statue where he appeared to be looking around. Then he moved back toward the camera. A moment later, he disappeared with one last statement, "Be back in a few." Apparently he felt his camera was hidden safely enough he could take a break.

Joy watched another few minutes of the video and realized the only action that was happening was the wind blowing through the trees on the other side of the statue. She checked the time remaining.

"I've only watched four minutes of this?" She groaned.

Her phone rang again. This time Joy looked down to see who was calling before she answered.

Evelyn.

"I have news," Evelyn said after Joy said hello. "I was able to use the markings on one of your photographs to find a file in the deep dark recesses of the file room."

"That's wonderful news." Joy put the phone on speaker and glanced at the computer screen. Thus far nothing had changed.

"I found blueprints that may help us. The drawing is from 1910, which is a little after the time period we've been looking at. I'm not an expert at drawings, but I think I see some areas where there could be extra space? The work was done when the building was fitted for gas lights, so this may be nothing at all, but I just can't tell. I wish I knew someone we could send this to."

"Like an architect?" Joy asked as she paused the video.

"Well, yes."

"What about Richard Bowe?" Joy suggested. "I just spoke to him about the remaining work that needs to be done on my remodel. We also talked about the statue. I can call him back to see if he would mind looking at the blueprints. Should I tell him to stop by your office?"

"Yes, that would be great. Give him both my cell and office numbers so we can arrange something."

"I'll call him when we're finished talking."

"Okay then, I'll make this fast. I found plenty on Alan Parker. Not only does he have a rap sheet for theft and a few other choice illegal activities, but he's also a missing person right now. He failed to show up at a hearing that kept being postponed. Finally the cops tried to find him, and he was gone. According to the news item I read, he's skipped the country. His passport was stamped in Mexico on Tuesday."

"Which means he couldn't have taken our statue. Not if he was in Mexico at the time."

"Right." Evelyn paused. "And I know we didn't talk about this, but I also did a search for Angela Simpson. The good news is I found plenty of people with that name."

"And the bad news?"

"The bad news is that none of them fit the age and description of the one currently employed by the hospital."

"So she's using a fake name?"

"The system isn't perfect," Evelyn said. "So it's possible I'm just not finding what I'm looking for. But I am suspicious."

"I got suspicious when she lied about going to the historical society."

They talked for a few more minutes, and then Joy hung up with Evelyn and scrolled in her recent calls list to click on Richard's name.

"Change your mind about the work, or did you find out the answer to the Ford or Butler question?" the architect said when he answered the phone.

"Actually, I've got a favor to ask."

"For you, anything, Joy. I've had several new clients come to me since I did the renovation for your place."

"I'm glad to hear it," Joy said. "This has to do with the hospital. We're looking into the question of whether secret rooms exist in the old wing of the hospital, and I wondered if you could help."

"I am a history buff, as you know. I'd love to help."

"We've found some drawings and blueprints that might shed some light on the question. Would you be interested in looking at what we've got? It would require meeting with Evelyn Perry in the records department at the hospital to view the evidence."

"You have me intrigued." He paused. "I wonder if she has time tomorrow."

"Let me give you her contact information. Then you can call her and make the arrangements."

"All right."

After she had provided Richard with the information, Joy thanked him again and hung up. Then she sent Evelyn a quick text to let her know he'd be reaching out to set up an appointment to view the documents.

Joy checked her watch. Her stomach was rumbling. She should make dinner. Just a few more minutes of watching the video, and she would head to the kitchen.

She turned back to the screen, her finger poised over the mouse. Then she spied the smudge of blue at the bottom of the frame.

She ran the video forward first at normal speed and then slowly to be sure of what she was seeing. She checked her watch again. Not yet five o'clock.

She dialed Angela's number. "I've got some errands to run in the morning. Do you mind opening the shop? I should be back by lunchtime. Lacy should be coming in by nine."

"It's fine, Mrs. A. I'm actually enjoying the added responsibility."

Joy said goodbye and then made two more calls. The first was to Evelyn. She didn't bother Anne, because this was her time of the day that she spent with Addie.

Then she called India Ainsworth-Brown.

Chapter Eighteen

THE NEXT MORNING, JOY AND Evelyn were ushered into the tastefully opulent St. John's Island home of India Ainsworth-Brown. India greeted them personally and directed them to a sunny sitting room where iced tea and hors d'oeuvres had been set out.

One wall was devoted to windows that overlooked the water while another was filled with books and knickknacks. Here and there plants of all sorts were fitted into the decorating scheme, making the room not only lovely but interesting.

"Thank you for seeing us so quickly," Evelyn said as they followed their hostess's lead and sat down on one of the two crimson-upholstered settees in the center of the room.

"How could I not?" India's voice was even and devoid of emotion. "I suppose you've brought it with you."

Joy nodded. "I can email the clip to you if you wish."

"That won't be necessary." India paused, her slender fingers worrying the strands of pearls at her wrist. "I believe you. Though I want you to show me, please."

"Yes, all right." Joy queued up the video on her phone and fast forwarded until she reached the moment of interest to India. Then she handed the phone to her.

India accepted the phone but placed it on the cushion next to her. Carefully she reached for one of the glasses of tea and lifted it to her lips. Parched after the drive, Joy did the same.

The sweet liquid soothed her thirst and made her smile. "There's lavender in here."

"Isn't it delicious? We grow it at our place in Texas. Near Fredericksburg. Have you been there?"

"Oh yes," Joy said. "When I lived in Houston, my husband and I loved to travel there, especially during bluebonnet season. Such a pretty area. I miss that."

"You're a widow."

A statement, not a question. Still Joy felt obliged to respond.

"Yes. Wilson died about eighteen months ago. I moved here to be near my daughter and her family."

"It's hard to be the one left behind," India said. "I don't think my Harold thought it through very well."

India shifted positions but made no move to pick up Joy's phone to view the video file. "I have a decent head for business, but I don't like it. That's why I bring Leticia to my events. She's good at those things. The organizational things." She paused. "I understand you met my sister, Leah."

The swift change of subject surprised Joy. "Yes I did," she said.

"We were once close, but she's allowed this issue with the hospital to make her bitter."

"Bitter enough to strike back?" Evelyn asked.

"Yes, actually, but not in the way you think." She drew a deep breath. "Leah was a benefactor to Mercy Hospital. Quietly to be sure, but she gave large amounts to have things improved or built. You see, our father left us both quite comfortable."

"I assume all of that stopped after her troubles with the surgery," Joy said.

India shrugged. "I love my sister, but she's stubborn. Even more so than I am. She had her mind made up how her treatment would progress, but things didn't happen that way. Had the doctor not operated, she might have died. Instead she's enjoying her revenge in the form of a budget crisis that she created. You'll be happy to know I've just hung up from a call with Garrison Baker. I'll be replenishing the funds that my sister has been denying Mercy Hospital."

"Garrison will be relieved," Evelyn said. "He's a good man who's shouldered a big load."

India nodded. "And Joy, Leah told me she emailed you and asked what you knew about Brown Construction and you gave us a nice review, which I appreciate. But she wasn't asking if you were satisfied with our work. She was warning you to look deeper into our company." Another pause. "Leah is loyal, but she has a strong sense of right and wrong. She also apparently knows my daughter better than I do."

At this, India reached for the phone and tapped the screen. Joy had watched that segment of the video enough times to know exactly what India was seeing.

When the clip was over, India handed the phone back to Joy. "Yes, that's her." Tears shimmered in her eyes. "Why would Leticia put one of my Noisettes on the statue? They weren't to be shown in public until I was certain the patent would go through." She studied Joy. "You've cultivated from those clippings, haven't you?"

"I've only gotten one to bloom. Now that I know the rose belongs to you, I'll bring the ones I've rooted back to you. It's the only right thing to do."

"Thank you," India said. "Again, though, why would my daughter do such a thing?"

"We wondered that too," Evelyn said. "Maybe you should ask her."

The doors opened, and Leticia stepped inside. "Were you eaves-dropping again?" India demanded. "It's a bad habit, and you really shouldn't—"

"You really don't understand why I put the roses on the statue?" Leticia's voice was tight, her tone strained. "You love those stupid flowers more than anything else in the world. They're all you ever talk about. And your battle over them with Claudia Guest. It's ridiculous."

"There's no battle," India said. "Claudia's roses are inferior. She hasn't been able to create a new variety for years."

"This isn't about Claudia at all. Just you. I figured if the secret got out about your precious rose, someone else might take the credit for it and you'd be baffled about how it happened. That was my goal in the beginning. But then when the statue was stolen and you found out your rose had been discovered, it was much more fun to watch you sweat. And to make you wonder how your secret blooms were showing up in such a public place."

"So you and Claudia Guest have been racing to patent a variety of rose?" Evelyn asked.

"Racing sounds so harsh. Let's say we were working together and then we weren't," said India.

"Because you're greedy," Leticia said. "Claudia was perfectly happy to continue—"

"Where is the statue, Leticia?"

Her mother's question temporarily silenced Leticia. Then she shook her head. "How should I know?"

"Because your boyfriend took it," Joy said calmly.

Leticia's face reddened. "I don't know what you're talking about."

"No?" Joy said. "I think you know exactly what we're talking about. You bought a baby gift for your boyfriend's sister in my gift shop. For Colin's sister."

Leticia sighed. "Yes, I did."

"You weren't the only one who was bent on getting even with someone in the family. Colin isn't happy with his aunt Claudia either. So although you were content to just pluck a rose from your mother's greenhouse and expose her secret bloom to the world, Colin had something bigger he was jealous of, didn't he?"

"The Angel of Mercy," India supplied, rolling her eyes. "Carved by an ancestor of Claudia Guest and paid for by another one. I've heard her tell the story ad nauseum, though I understand there might be another side to that story. So imagine how much more Colin heard it."

When Leticia didn't deny her allegation, Joy knew their hunch was correct. "Leticia, you haven't asked how we found out it was you putting the flowers on the statue," she said.

"Does it matter?" she asked.

"When you learn how we discovered your secret, it will." Joy picked up her phone and re-queued the video that India had seen. Then she hit PLAY and handed the phone to Leticia.

She knew the video was close to the end when she heard the familiar female voice. "Just give me a minute to leave this." Seconds later Leticia put the phone down.

"Leticia, you've already admitted you placed the roses on the statue," Evelyn said. "And we have evidence that you and someone else were there the night it was stolen. I'm betting that person was Colin. How do we know y'all didn't take it?"

Leticia looked as if she might answer. Then she closed her mouth.

India shook her head. "I know that's Leticia's voice," she said, "but I don't see any evidence that she was there to steal anything. Is it possible she showed up to place a Noisette on the base and scared off the thief?"

"Yes," Evelyn said, "that's possible. But what about the photograph that Colin showed Joy? The one taken in her garage?"

Leticia shrugged. "He told me about that. What about it?"

"You gave him the key that the Brown Construction workmen used during renovations, didn't you?" Joy asked. "We never wrapped up the final punch list of detail work, something that Richard Bowe reminded me of just today. Great timing on his part, wouldn't you say? I wouldn't have made the connection without that reminder that the workmen weren't done and hadn't given me back the key to my garage. I'm guessing that Colin lied to me about his aunt taking the picture of my rose and that he's the one who did."

Leticia stared at her but continued to remain silent. India, however, wiped a tear that traced a path down her cheek.

"I believe you have your answer," Evelyn said.

"Colin works at Brown Construction," Leticia said, a hitch in her voice. "So yes, he's visited my office. But I've never given him a key to a client's property. However, you may be right in saying he took one."

"Ladies," India said gently, "I regret that trouble between my daughter and me has spilled out into such a public arena. She's admitted to placing the Noisettes on the statue's base and, unfortunately, we now know the reason for that." She paused. "Under the circumstances, and without any concrete proof that she was involved in the theft, I am going to have to ask you to leave us to settle this issue in private."

"Leticia," Joy said, ignoring India's plea, "did you take the statue?"

"No!" she said vehemently. "It wasn't me."

"Did Colin?" Evelyn asked.

"No," she said then she hesitated. "I don't think so, anyway."

The ladies exchanged looks. "What do you mean?" India asked before any of them could.

"I was there to leave a rose. You're right, Colin came with me. I left the rose, and then he took me home."

"What time was that?" Joy asked her.

"I don't know," she said. "Truly. I wasn't paying attention. Colin and I ... well, we had a fight right before we got to the hospital, so I wasn't speaking to him." Leticia was quiet for a moment. "Other than what you heard there, I probably didn't say much more than that on the whole drive to my house."

"What were you fighting over?" Evelyn asked.

"I'd rather not say," Leticia said.

India sighed. "All right. I think we're done for today." She captured Joy's gaze. "Thank you for bringing all of this to my attention. And for agreeing to return the rose cuttings. I appreciate that more than you can know. Now why don't I walk you out?"

Joy offered a smile and fell into step beside India. Evelyn followed behind them. At the door, India hesitated. Her look was pleading, her expression sober. "If you find out she's lying, will you tell me before the police are told?"

"I can't promise that," Joy said, clutching her phone.

"Then let's hope she's telling the truth."

Joy stepped away from the door and stumbled on the step. Her phone went tumbling down along with her.

Evelyn retrieved the phone. "Are you all right?" she asked.

"Just bruised my pride," she said, righting herself. "Have I ruined my phone?"

Evelyn held the phone in her palm. "I think you've just turned it off. Hit the button maybe?" She pressed the button on the side of the phone, and it began to power back on. "Let's get back to the car," she said. "And watch your step."

Joy settled into the passenger seat of Evelyn's car. She would have a bruise or two tomorrow, but at least she hadn't broken anything.

Her phone jangled with the sound it always made when it turned on. Then came a ding indicating she had a text.

It was a video clip from a number she didn't recognize, with a message that read SHE'S HERE.

"Hold on, Evelyn," Joy said as she clicked the icon to start the video. "Let's see what this shows first."

They sat in silence while the video began to play. The clip wasn't long, maybe two or three minutes, but what it showed was fascinating.

Joy closed out the video and made a call. "Detective Osborne," she said when the woman's voice came on the line, "we know where the Angel of Mercy statue is."

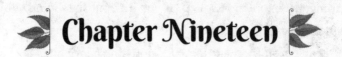

Chapter Nineteen

BY THE TIME JOY AND Evelyn arrived at the hospital, after making a quick stop to pick up Anne from her home, the place was crawling with police. The friends found Detective Osborne standing in the lobby speaking with a half-dozen uniformed officers.

"You got here pretty quickly," Joy said to the detective.

"You said the angel was here."

Joy shook her head. "Not here in the lobby. But near."

"Come on," Evelyn said. "We'll show you."

She and Joy led the way back outside and around to the south side of the building where Norm had been conked on the head. They walked along the wall behind the hedge until they were opposite the magnolia tree. Then Joy got down on her hands and knees and carefully ran her hands over the grass, searching for a seam in the turf.

After a few anxious minutes, she found it—a slight rise above the surrounding sod. She ran her hand along the seam until she found the corner.

Joy stood and beckoned to the detective. "Detective Osborne, could you have a couple of officers lift this section of grass?"

Two young men squeezed forward, and in a matter of minutes they'd gotten their arms under the heavy section of sod and moved it to one side. Joy estimated it to be about four square feet. Then they lifted out a wooden plank that rested on a frame and supported the sod.

Joy peered down into a shaft that went straight down, with rungs on one side like a ladder mounted in the bricks that lined it. She breathed a sigh of relief then spoke over her shoulder.

"There she is."

"So it never left the property," Detective Osborne said. "How about that?"

"Yes how about that?" Anne pressed past them to kneel down and peer at the statue standing below them. The top of her head was just past an arm's length away. "I can't believe we actually found her."

"Don't touch anything," the detective said.

Anne sprang up. "I'm sorry. I just, well, I'm so glad to see her again. I didn't think I'd be so emotional about a silly statue."

Joy wiped away a tear. "I feel the same."

"I'm sorry, but we're going to have to secure this area," Detective Osborne told them. "It's a crime scene now."

"Would you mind if I took a picture first?" Joy asked. "Just for me and not to distribute."

The detective nodded. "Just one, and then I'll have to insist you go back inside."

"Thank you," Joy said as she retrieved her phone, leaned over, and took a photograph of the angel. She straightened to face the detective. "When will she be back in place?"

"She'll go to the crime lab first. Then once we're sure we've got what we need, the statue will be returned to her spot. Shouldn't take more than a day."

On Thursday morning Joy made her way past the empty base where the statue would soon be placed once again and then returned to the front of the hospital and entered the lobby. She found the door to the gift shop open and lights on inside.

Had she not seen Garrison Baker pouring coffee into two mugs, she might have been concerned. "Taking me up on my offer to help yourself, I see," she said as she stepped inside and placed the bundle of flowers from her garden on the counter.

"You've earned this coffee." He smiled. "And more. I may just be able to give you a raise. It looks like our budget has been wrangled into submission thanks to not one benefactor but three."

"Is that right?" Joy accepted the mug Garrison handed her and took a sip. "Who are they? Can you say?"

"I can. India Ainsworth is a new donor, and her sister Leah has renewed her giving. Do you know Roger Gaylord?"

"Who in Charleston doesn't? He's on several boards and donates to many worthy causes."

"Including Mercy Hospital," Garrison said. "He told me he had no idea we were in need until he saw the piece about the statue and looked into things. So three donors in one day. That's a miracle." He took a sip from his mug. "And of course, there's the miracle of the secret hiding place you found."

"I wouldn't say I found it," Joy said modestly. "I wish they could figure out who sent me that video though." She put her mug on the counter. "Have the police been able to figure out anything about it? Is it really just a hole, or is there more to it than that?"

"It's much more than just a hole," Garrison said. "When they got the angel out, they could see that there was an opening that led to a passageway underneath the hospital. It only goes about twenty feet, and then there's another opening above that leads to a trap door in—"

"The Vault!" Joy cried. "Evelyn must be tickled pink. Not only with the thought of a secret passage right under her feet, but she's been wanting to replace that awful carpeting for years, she told me."

"Yes," Garrison said, "Evelyn is 'tickled pink,' as you say."

"Speaking of miracles," Joy said, nodding toward the front double doors that Angela Simpson was about to walk through. "Who is she really, and why did someone pay the hospital to hire her?"

"I'm not at liberty to say," Garrison said, "but I hope she's welcome here at the gift shop."

"Yes, I've been very pleased with her. She always seems to know just what a customer wants, sometimes even before the customer tells her. It's as if she knows what they're thinking. Or at least knows what they need." Joy shook her head. "I'm not expressing it well."

"I've heard that from others too, besides that she looks so much like the statue." He paused. "Speaking of the statue, arrangements are being made for it to be reset tomorrow morning. We're trying to get it done before the bad weather hits. I'm encouraging all staff who can to attend."

"Before the hurricane hits?" she said. "Wouldn't it be better to wait until after?"

"If a hurricane is going to hit Charleston, I want to take every precaution, including having our angel back where she belongs."

"I'm just glad she's back." Joy looked up at the clock. "I wonder why Angela is here so early. Her shift doesn't begin for another hour."

"She's here to meet me. Apparently she's found something to add to the maps on my wall. And more, I think, though I don't know what else she has." He put his mug down and waved to Angela, who was now watching them. "I guess I'm about to find out."

He stepped out into the lobby, and a moment later the two of them passed Anne, headed toward the elevators.

Anne came in smiling. "What are those two up to?"

"I have no idea," Joy told her. "Come in the back and have coffee if you've got time."

"I do," she said. "I've been wondering what's happening with the investigation. Do they have any idea at all who sent you that text?"

"They don't," Joy said. "They took my phone to see what they could get from it, and I only got it back this morning. As far as I know, they haven't figured out who sent the text, but then, I don't know how those things work." She sighed. "The good news is the angel is back."

"Agreed," Anne said as she accepted a mug of coffee from Joy. "But I do wonder why in the world someone went to the trouble to steal the statue only to put it in a hole in the ground."

"Maybe they were waiting for a good time to dispose of it," Anne offered.

"But how were they going to dispose of it?" Joy took a sip of her coffee then set her mug down. "And why didn't they? Why in the world did they tell me where it was?"

At half past ten on Friday morning, Garrison Baker and a collection of local dignitaries cut the ribbon that draped across the newly returned Angel of Mercy statue. Joy had closed the gift shop in honor of the moment and now stood beside Angela and Shirley near the statue's base. Anne and Evelyn had taken places directly behind them.

Television cameras and lights had been set up to film the occasion. Bailey Carver held her microphone at her side, likely waiting for the videographer to move his focus from the ceremony to her. Other reporters were doing the same.

Garrison stepped up to the podium last after other civic leaders had expounded on their delight that the statue was back in her spot at Mercy Hospital. Before he said anything, he turned toward the statue then looked back at the cameras. "Doesn't she look beautiful?"

After a round of applause and one shrill wolf whistle from somewhere in the crowd, the audience quieted. Then Garrison smiled.

"You know the history of this statue, and we've talked about how she returned. I would like to once again extend my thanks to Detective Osborne and her staff. From what the detective has told me, she had help from a few members of the hospital staff. Joy Atkins, Anne Mabry, and Evelyn Perry, where are you?"

"Oh my goodness," Anne said. "That's so nice of him."

The ladies waved, and once again the audience clapped. As Joy looked around, she spied Claudia Guest. Their gazes collided, and Claudia smiled. A moment later, she began moving toward Joy through the crowd.

"She's beautiful up there, isn't she?" Joy said when Claudia arrived at her side.

Claudia wore a red sheath dress with matching flats. At her neck was a single strand of perfectly matched white pearls, each the size of a marble. Dark glasses and ruby red lipstick completed her look.

"Yes she is. I'm happy she's returned, but I will use all of my influence as a Butler descendant to move her to a place of safety so this sort of thing doesn't happen again." She paused. "We paid for that statue, you know. Probably carved it too."

Joy nodded but decided to change the subject. "Claudia, I saw Colin outside my house on Monday. He had a picture on his phone that he said he took from you. It was a picture of India's Noisette I was propagating in my garage. Do you know how he knew it was there?"

Claudia looked sad but resigned. "I don't know," she said. "And I don't know why he would try to turn you against me. I raised him like a son since the age of twelve. He arrived on my doorstep angry, and I haven't always been able to break through to him. He has his moments, and I have mine. We'll work out our differences. We always have."

"I hope so." Joy returned her attention to Garrison.

"In honor of the Angel of Mercy's return, we have not one special guest here, but two. The first is bestselling author and noted authority on roses, Charleston's own India Ainsworth-Brown."

The crowd parted, and India emerged wearing almost an identical red ensemble to the one Claudia had donned. The difference was India's choice to accent with diamonds instead of pearls. Following in her mother's wake was a nervous-looking Leticia Brown. Most surprising of all, in Leticia's arms was a bouquet of white Noisette roses with red centers.

"I'll be brief," India said after the microphone had been adjusted to fit her height. "My daughter and I would like to give our gift to the city, to Mercy Hospital, and to the Angel of Mercy in honor of the statue's return." She gestured to Leticia.

Leticia formed what might pass as a smile, and she clutched the bouquet as if her life depended on it.

Joy had heard through the grapevine that Leticia and Colin would likely not be charged in the statue's disappearance. There was no proof she'd done anything other than place the rose there. There was also no proof—*yet,* as Detective Osborne said—as to who actually took the statue. However, she held out hope that the culprit would be caught very soon.

India offered a smile to Garrison. "So please accept the first dozen of many Angel of Mercy Noisette roses." She returned her attention to Leticia. "And don't be surprised if one occasionally shows up at the feet of the statue. It's a lovely way to honor her, isn't it? Oh, and don't forget to buy my latest book. We're rushing an updated version to print with details of the Angel of Mercy Noisette. Preorders are up to buy now."

At her mother's nod, Leticia took one of the roses from the bundle and handed the rest to Garrison. Cameras followed as Leticia then walked over to the statue and placed a rose on the base at the angel's feet.

Claudia leaned close. "Oh, she's good. She turned this whole thing into a gesture of her goodwill and a publicity stunt to promote her new book. I've got to hand it to her even if I am devastated that she beat me to the cultivation of those Noisettes."

India smiled at the crowd and made her exit with Leticia following. Then Garrison stepped back up and placed the bundle of Noisettes on the podium. "Thank you, India. Now I have one more special guest. This one will be a surprise to those of you who know her as an employee of the hospital."

He paused to look in Joy's direction.

"Please welcome Angela Simpson."

"Angela?" Joy looked at her part-time shop clerk who still stood beside her. "This is certainly a surprise." She watched Angela make her way to the podium.

"Oh my," Claudia said. "She looks exactly like the angel, doesn't she?"

Joy nodded, keeping her attention focused on her assistant. When Angela reached the podium, Garrison moved over to allow her to stand in front of the microphone.

"As Mr. Baker and the others have said, we're here to welcome the Angel of Mercy back home where she belongs. Well, here's the thing. I'm kind of like that statue." She paused to smile. "See, when I came to Charleston, I was coming home where I belonged too. For those of you who don't know me, I was adopted as an infant and have been looking for my history for a while now. My adoptive mother was given very little information about me, but she did have a name, Mercy Hospital, Charleston, South Carolina. She was also given a locket with a key and a tiny painted portrait inside it. That was the beginning of my search for who I am. Standing here in front of you brings me to the end of that search."

Several cameras flashed, breaking the silence that fell. Out on the street, a car rolled past.

"Some of you have noticed that I bear a resemblance to the Angel of Mercy. There's a reason for that." Again she paused, this time searching out Joy's face in the crowd and giving her a smile. "It took some doing, but I got confirmation this week—thanks to a key that opened a safe deposit box that hadn't been opened for more than eighty years—that I am a descendant of the woman who posed for this statue and also for the portrait in my locket. Her name was Mercy. Mercy Ford. Isn't that cool?"

A murmuring went up in the crowd. Joy felt Claudia stiffen beside her.

"You know who Mercy Ford is, don't you?" she asked Claudia.

"I'm afraid so," she whispered.

"The papers in the box, including old maps that Mr. Baker will be framing for his office, show that Mercy Ford paid for the statue herself after she was left at the altar by a man named Butler. She was heartbroken but couldn't resist leaving something of herself when she left town. So she commissioned this statue, saw it to completion, and then disappeared from Charleston. After tracing my family tree backward, here I am."

Garrison stepped up to the microphone. "You'll be happy to know that a book about Mercy Ford and how the statue came to be here is in the works based on the papers that Angela found in that safe deposit box. For that we can thank India Ainsworth-Brown, who is not only the person funding the project but also the author."

"That figures," Claudia muttered.

"So without any further ado," Garrison said, "let's have the third great-granddaughter of Mercy Ford cut the ribbon on the Angel of Mercy."

Claudia leaned over. "I can't bear to watch any more of this. However," she said gently, "I'm glad that girl found her home. Charleston always seems to bring its own home, doesn't it?"

"I got here as quickly as I could," Joy said with a smile. "See you at the next garden club meeting?"

"Absolutely," Claudia said. "I've been working on a new variety of Noisettes, and I may as well bring samples. There's no point in hiding them."

"I look forward to seeing them," Joy said as applause went up around them.

Claudia disappeared into the crowd. A few minutes later, the ceremony ended. As the press swarmed those still circling the podium, Joy edged her way toward the statue.

"It's good to have you back," she whispered. She ran her hand over the statue's foot and winked up at her.

Something was wrong.

Joy reached again to run her hand over the left foot of the statue. She felt nothing but smooth, flawless stone.

She turned to see Anne and Evelyn moving her way.

"What's wrong?" Anne demanded.

"You look like you've seen a ghost," Evelyn said.

"Not a ghost." She looked up at the statue and then back at her friends. "But I do see a fake. This is not the real Angel of Mercy."

Chapter Twenty

HER HANDS SHAKING, JOY RETURNED to the gift shop. She managed to get the key in the lock on the third attempt. Anne and Evelyn followed her inside and into the back room.

"You're certain?" Evelyn said.

"Absolutely," Joy told her. "Every morning when I pass the statue, I pat her foot. I know it's silly, but it's just a physical connection that feels good."

"I understand that," Evelyn said. "Lots of people do things like that."

"Anyway," Joy continued, "there's a groove on the statue's left foot that isn't there anymore. I could understand if she was damaged in moving her and something was broken off, but there's no way to explain missing parts filled in."

Anne clasped her hands together. "We need to tell someone."

"I doubt we'll be believed," Joy said. "Not when the return of the statue has been played up with such fanfare."

"And a book is going to be written about it," Evelyn added. "Did you have any idea that's what Angela was up to?"

"None," Joy said. "Angela didn't say a word about why she was here. It does make me think that India might be the person who paid for her to work here. But why?"

"So Angela would return," Anne said. "There's no book without the person who has all the documentation."

"Right, but how did India know about the safe deposit box and Angela?" Evelyn asked.

"Good question." Joy shrugged. "Okay, I think we need to do some searching for the real statue before we alert anyone to the fact that they've got the wrong Angel of Mercy out in front of the hospital. Unfortunately, I can't leave to go anywhere until after I close the shop this afternoon."

"And I'm in the same situation," Evelyn said. "We've got a staff meeting and lunch, and then I'm having my employees work on special projects. I need to be there to supervise."

Anne smiled. "The good news is, I'm not volunteering today, so I don't mind doing some legwork on this. The question is where to begin."

"I'll leave you to it, then," Evelyn said. "Keep me posted. I'll check in with you when my workday is over."

With that, Evelyn made her way out of the store. The bell jingled as the door closed behind her.

Joy gave Anne's question about where to begin a moment's thought. "We already have proof that Leticia and Colin were at the statue. Leticia claims Colin took her home. She even said she doesn't think he did it, but she didn't say she was certain of it."

"True," Anne said. "So if Colin is our suspect, then he's either hidden the real statue or sold it." She frowned. "I'm afraid it's the latter."

"Okay, if he sold it then to whom?" Joy paused. "He's Claudia Guest's nephew, and thus a member of the Butler clan. I'm guessing he could make a bundle if he found the right rich relation proud enough to want to own it even if they couldn't have bragging rights. How about you go see Claudia and ask her who in their family might want to own the statue. She might be reluctant to talk about it at first, but if you tell her about the fake statue, I think she'll cooperate. Claudia really does love that statue, no matter which family donated it to the city."

Joy paused. "Another thing we have to consider is that Colin might still be hiding it for some reason. But where would he keep it?"

"Let's think on that, shall we?" Anne said as the shop door opened.

Joy nodded and then stepped out of the back room with Anne behind her. "Angela," Joy said. "Congratulations. You had quite an unveiling out there."

"Thank you. It was very exciting." Angela's eyes were shining. "I'm sorry I had to keep a secret from you, Mrs. A. Mr. Baker told me I needed to keep quiet about everything until the ceremony."

Anne said her goodbyes and left. Joy waited until she was gone and then beckoned to Angela to join her in the back room. "How long have you known all of this?"

"I didn't know all of it until two days ago. I had no idea what the key fit."

"How did you find that out?"

"See, that's what's interesting. I met this guy—he's really cute and really nice—and he asked me if I wanted to be in a video game. I thought he was joking, then I thought maybe he was trying to feed me a line, you know. Some guys will tell you anything to date you."

"But he was telling the truth," Joy said. "And would I be right if I guessed his name is Liam Sterling?"

Angela's mouth fell open. "How did you know?"

"We've met," she said. "His brother is marrying a nurse who works in the maternity ward."

"Well, Liam is making this video game about the statue being stolen—which you probably know if you know all the other stuff—and he thought it would be cool if he could animate the statue. And it turned out to be super cool. He had me stand in front of a green screen in an outfit like Mercy Ford's. He's going to have Mercy—the statue—walking around in the hospital and coming in and out of secret passageways."

Joy had to admit that sounded interesting. "What does that have to do with how you found the papers?"

"He saw the key and recognized it right away as being a safe deposit key. He said he could find out what bank issued the key. I didn't ask him how, but he's good with computers, so maybe he researched it online. Anyway, he gave me the name of the bank, and I went there to see what was in the box. But the instructions on the box said that it could only be opened by a Ford heir, so I had to first get someone to vouch for how I got the key and who I was and, well, it's a long story, but the historical society folks took one look at my locket and the paper trail I'd found that led me to Charleston and they were willing to write a letter to the bank stating that I was a Ford heir."

"How did that not get around? I've heard more than once that Charleston is a big city and yet a small one." Joy smiled. "I even heard it from my assistant."

"It was all very confidential, I guess," Angela said. "The bank made the call, so I just went where I was told."

"How long have you known India Ainsworth-Brown?"

Angela looked away and seemed to be considering her response. "About six months, maybe more. See, Mrs. Brown found me. She's the person who gave me the paper trail I told you about."

"So India was determined to find a Ford heir."

"And she did," Angela said.

Anything to one-up her rival, Claudia Guest.

A thought occurred. "What do you know about a second statue?"

Angela frowned. "What do you mean?"

"Liam was making a video game. Did he order a second statue for the game?"

She shook her head. "I don't think so. At least he never mentioned it if he did. I mean, wouldn't that be expensive?"

"Probably," Joy said as the door opened.

"That'll be Mr. Dennis. He's due to replace the flowers on his wife's bedside." She paused. "She's in the memory care unit."

Angela stepped out into the store. "Hello there, Mr. Dennis. I put together a bouquet for you to bring to your wife." She went to the refrigerated display case and took out a beautiful arrangement.

Joy moved to the door to see the elderly man's face light up. "Thank you, Angela."

Then his lip trembled. Something was wrong. Before Joy could speak, he continued.

"They're purple irises," he said, his voice wavering. "How did you ... that is, how could you know? My wife has been nonverbal since her last stroke. She couldn't have told you."

"Know what?" Joy asked, joining them at the counter.

"My wife carried purple irises in our wedding." Tears swam in his eyes as he looked first to Joy then to Angela. "Today is our sixty-second anniversary."

He retrieved his handkerchief and dabbed at his eyes then paid for the flowers and left, a trail of thank-yous following him to the door. Once he'd gone, Joy turned to Angela.

"How *did* you know?"

"Mrs. Dennis told me," she said. "So, should I go ahead and make the deliveries, or do you have something else for me to do?"

"No," Joy said slowly, "but Mr. Dennis said his wife is nonverbal. How could she tell you that irises were her favorite flower?"

Angela smiled. "I wish I could explain how I knew. All I can say is that she told me, just not with words. It happens like that with me sometimes. I just know things."

Joy matched her grin. "Well, okay. Then go ahead and make those deliveries."

The rest of the day flew by, as once the news team had their stories they were keen to get a view inside the hospital too. Since security guards employed for the event kept the media confined to the first floor, many of them ended up either in the gift shop or the café.

During a brief lull, Joy picked up the phone to call Liam Sterling. "Do you have a minute to answer a question?" she asked him when he answered.

"Sure. What's up?"

"Angela told me you've been working together."

"Yeah, is that the question?" Liam asked.

"No," she told him. "The question is whether you had any other props for the videos you've been shooting. Say another statue?"

"What do you mean?"

"Did you have a life-size copy of the Angel of Mercy made?"

He chuckled. "No way, Mrs. Atkins. That would be pricey, and I am strictly a low-budget dude. Just me, my laptop, and my GoPro."

"Your GoPro?"

"It's a camera that straps onto something—I wear it on my chest, usually, or my hat—and it films things. The quality isn't always the best, but it does simulate a person walking, and it picks up sounds pretty well."

"Were you wearing a GoPro the night you took the video that you shared with me?"

"I was wearing it except for when I took it off and shoved it into the hedge," he said. "But yeah, I'm usually wearing it when I film. I set it to be sound activated so I don't have to think about turning it off and on."

"Have you looked at any more footage from the night the statue was stolen?"

"The GoPro footage?" he asked. "Nope. When I got home the battery had run down. I'd forgotten to charge it, so I didn't capture anything else with it."

"When was that, exactly? That Leticia showed up, I mean."

"Dunno," he told her. "You'd have to look at the time stamp." Then he paused. "Mrs. Atkins, there is one more thing I thought of. I don't know if it'll help, but I told the police when they interviewed me."

Joy raised her eyebrows. "What's that?"

209

"When I was getting my camera and packing up that night, I saw two guys getting out of a black pickup parked on the street. The only reason I thought it was odd is that one of them was wearing a cape. I thought that was cool. In fact, when I revamped the game to take into account how long the statue removal was, I gave one of the bad guys a cape."

"Could you give me a description?" Joy asked.

"Average height and weight, both of them," he said. "Just normal, you know?"

Joy thought of one more thing. "Liam, have you ever skateboarded inside the hospital?"

She heard a sheepish chuckle. "I might have done that a time or two. I wanted footage for the game of zooming down a hallway."

"I'm going to assume you got what you needed and won't be repeating it, so there's no need for me to mention it to anyone?"

"I think you could safely assume that." He cleared his throat. "And thanks, Mrs. Atkins."

"You'll tell me if you remember anything else, won't you?"

He agreed, and they said their goodbyes. Joy tucked her phone into her pocket. Two men, one of them wearing a cape. Now that was news.

But who were they?

Chapter Twenty-One

JOY MET EVELYN IN THE hospital parking lot. They had one mission this afternoon—to speak to Colin Guest. Joy didn't hold out much hope that she could get him to talk, but she couldn't let the opportunity go by without trying.

"Anne's trying to track down Claudia," Joy began after they were on their way. "She said she'd call when she's free and join us. However, I have news."

"Okay, what news?"

She relayed Liam's story about the two men.

"Why didn't he tell us that before?" Evelyn asked. "All this time I've been thinking it must have been Colin and Leticia."

"It might have been," Joy said. "But then again, it might not have been."

Evelyn sat back against the seat and let out a long breath. "Somewhere out there is the Angel of Mercy, and someone knows where it is."

"Well, it isn't Liam Sterling."

"You're certain?" Evelyn asked.

"I questioned him at length, and I'm convinced he doesn't know."

Joy turned on East Bay Street and pulled her car to a stop at the entrance to the alley behind Candles & Curiosities Emporium. Then she eased forward until the Mini was parked behind the art studio.

Together they walked toward the door.

"Can anyone just go inside?" Evelyn asked. "Isn't the door ever locked?"

"I think they can. Mallory and I were with Flavia, though, so I'm not sure. Let's see." She opened the door and stepped into the studio with Evelyn on her heels. "Okay, so the answer is apparently yes."

As before, the place was a hive of activity. The first person to greet her was Ace, the glassblower whose grandmother was a patient at Mercy Hospital.

"Mrs. Atkins," she said. "Good to see you. I've been meaning to come down and talk to you about that girl you've got working for you."

"Angela or Lacy?" she said. "Those are my regulars."

"Angela. I showed up to the hospital to visit, and there she was sitting on the floor with my mother."

"On the floor?" Joy shook her head. "I am sorry. She shouldn't have done that."

"No, you don't understand. Mama wanted to play jacks. She thinks sometimes that she's still a kid. But who can find jacks anywhere? So there she was, sitting on the floor with my mother, playing jacks." Ace shook her head. "It was the craziest thing. Because I hadn't told her I had given up on finding them."

"She just knew," Joy said.

"Yeah, exactly. Anyway, I thought I'd tell you how much I appreciate her."

"I'll pass that on." She paused. "Have you seen Colin Guest around?"

"He was here earlier, but he's not here now," she said.

"Do you know what he's been working on lately? I'm curious if you've seen him carving any statues that look like the Angel of Mercy."

She shook her head. "Not his thing. He tends to stay away from anything related to his family in his art."

"He told you that?"

"He tells everyone that," Ace said. "I never asked why. His aunt seems like a nice lady."

"She is," Joy said.

"She was looking for him too." Ace shrugged. "She might still be in his studio. Do you remember where it is?"

"Claudia is here?" Joy looked back at Evelyn then returned her attention to Ace. "Thanks for telling us. And I'll be sure to pass your message on to Angela."

After sending a text to Anne to let her know they'd found Claudia, Joy led Evelyn through the maze of hallways until she reached Colin's studio. Indeed, there was Claudia, seated on a rough wooden bench, her head in her hands.

"Claudia," Joy said. "What are you doing here?"

"Waiting for Colin," she said when she looked up. "I figure he'll show up eventually."

Joy and Evelyn exchanged looks.

"He seems angry with you," Evelyn said. "Do you think he'll listen?"

Joy walked over to press her hand on Claudia's shoulder. "Is there anything I can do?"

She looked up with grateful eyes. "I wish. Thank you. I know we haven't known each other very long, but I think we could be friends.

Though I did come on awfully strong at the beginning, what with insisting you come to the garden club meetings."

Joy chuckled. "It's all worked out fine. I actually enjoyed the last meeting."

"I didn't," Claudia muttered, "though I suppose India and I will need to make peace too. I've been a bit pushy about the fact that I thought my family was responsible for the Angel of Mercy. But now that I see that isn't the case, well, I cringe when I think of how I have behaved."

Joy squeezed her shoulder. "The Lord's mercies are new every morning," she said. "For that I'm thankful. There's nothing shameful in starting over. And talking with Colin is a good start."

She looked over at Evelyn. "We can stay until he arrives."

"That won't be necessary."

"Joy," Evelyn said, "we might want to take a peek around just to make sure there aren't any traces of what we're looking for."

"Good idea." Joy looked at Claudia. "Do you mind if we look around Colin's studio?"

"Not at all," Claudia said.

Joy and Evelyn performed a thorough search and came up empty. "Are you sure you'll be okay, Claudia?"

"Positive," she said.

"I hope your conversation achieves what you want it to," she said.

"And I hope you find whatever it is you're looking for," Claudia told them.

"Actually we're looking for a second Angel of Mercy statue," Evelyn said. "You haven't seen one, have you?"

"I have, actually. I was told it was a prop for a performance."

"Well," Evelyn said casually, "It probably was. Where exactly did you see it?"

"I'll give you the address," Claudia said. "It's adjacent to the Brown Construction property out on the highway. Do you know the area?"

"I do. So how did you come to see this prop statue?" Joy asked.

"I'd gone to try to convince my sister to speak to Colin. He wasn't listening to me so I thought … I hoped …" She paused to retrieve her phone. A moment later she finished typing and looked up. "I sent you the address. Anyway, I was on a mission to repair my relationship with Colin. I didn't pay much attention to anything else while I was there."

Joy's phone dinged with a text. She offered Claudia a smile.

"Thank you."

They walked out to the car and climbed in. Joy opened her texts. CHARLESTON COSTUME WAREHOUSE AND THEATER SERVICES. She input the address into the GPS and set off.

They rode in silence until their location came into view.

"So we're just going to walk in and ask to see the Angel of Mercy statue?" Evelyn asked.

"Why not?" Joy said with a smile.

Once inside the warehouse—which was every bit as expansive as the name implied—Joy found a sales clerk and asked for a replica of the statue. A dark-haired woman looked up from her magazine, peering at them over the tops of turquoise leopard reading glasses.

"We do have one," she said. "Let's go look. I never know what's been rented out from one day to the next."

They stepped into a cavernous wonderland of costumes, set pieces, and other items to fill any theater need. "That's odd," she said, stopping abruptly. "It was right there yesterday. Let me go check the books."

"Do you mind if we look around?" Evelyn called after her. "We might find something we need."

"Sure go ahead."

"Do we split up or stick together?" Evelyn asked.

"Let's split up. Keep your phone handy, and let me know if you find anything. I'll do the same."

Joy set off in one direction and Evelyn the other. She combed rows of items of all sorts, ending up at the far wall of the building. A door stood ajar, so she glanced inside the room beyond.

An old wooden desk was strewn with piles of costumes. Random pieces of sets were stacked behind it, preventing a view of the rest of the room. She reached around for a light and found the switch. She flipped it, and the storeroom was ablaze with lights.

Joy wandered past the costumes and set pieces to see what might be behind them. There on the back wall was what looked like a ghost standing in front of a closed garage door. The figure was slightly smaller than Joy in height and had been shrouded with painter's cloth or perhaps old sheets.

She moved toward it. Then she tugged at the cloth.

The fabric fell away, revealing an Angel of Mercy statue.

"Oh, hi, Joy. Can I help you?"

Joy whirled around to see Norm Ashford standing there. She smiled.

"I'm sorry," she said. "Curiosity got the better of me. Are you working a side job here?"

"Something like that," he said.

"Any idea where this statue came from?"

He nodded. "It's a copy of the one that got put back up today," he said. "I believe they're using it in the *Night at the Museum* performance. Or were. It's been canceled because of the storm."

"So I heard." She turned to run her hand over the smooth stone. Then she looked down and ran her hand over the angel's left foot. Her heart started to race when she felt the familiar groove.

She slowly turned back to Norm. "This statue was stolen. It's the original Angel of Mercy."

He shook his head. "It's a good copy," he told her. "The set guys here are talented. Colin Guest does a lot of the work. His stuff ought to be in a museum."

"Maybe it will be someday," she said. "But right now, his work is bolted to the base in front of Mercy Hospital. And the original statue is right here."

He sighed again. "I really wish you'd minded your own business, Joy."

In that moment she realized what she'd been missing all along. Norm Ashford was involved in the theft. Of course.

How involved remained to be seen.

"Who did this, Norm? You're not a thief. Who paid you to look away?"

His expression never changed. "Now Joy, I can't tell you that. You're a nice lady, and you don't need to be involved in this. How about we forget we ever had this conversation? The statue on the base is the Angel of Mercy. It's been decided and repositioned there. No one has to know. Just walk out now."

"I will know, Norm," she said. "And so will you."

Silence fell between them.

"The thief hit you on the head, at least that was your story. Did that really happen, and was it part of the plan?"

He paused only an instant. "It really did happen, and it wasn't part of the plan. I accepted the offer of a little under the table payment, but then I regretted it. Tried to give it back. I had second thoughts, you know? I was never a bad cop, so why start in my retirement?"

"Second thoughts?"

"He offered me a lot of money," Norm said. "I was stupid and thought I could use it to help at the church. But I came to my senses fast and had a talk with my pastor about it. He told me to go to the police, which I should have done immediately. But I thought maybe I could fix it myself."

"How were you going to do that?" Joy asked him.

"Arrest him. I had my handcuffs with me. I figure a man can't steal a statue if he doesn't have use of his hands."

"But he snuck up on you and hit you on the back of the head," Joy said. "Is that how that bump happened?"

"We argued," Norm said. "I couldn't just cuff him and call the cops. It would be his word against mine, and with the evidence he had against me, it wouldn't look good."

"Then how did you come to take a blow to the back of your head?" Evelyn had joined them, moving from the door to join Norm inside the storeroom.

"I was helping him," Norm said. "I know how that sounds, but I'm telling you I was just waiting for him to do the deed. After we got the real statue in the pickup and the fake statue in its hiding place, I told him I was gonna turn him in." He looked down at the floor. "I lied about the flatbed truck and the front loader. And about calling Mr. Baker. All we needed was a pickup. We could handle carrying the statue."

Norm's voice was shaking when he said, "Look, someone will be coming for that thing anytime now. Let's all just walk out of here and close the door behind us, okay? We can talk somewhere safe."

"Who's coming for it?"

"Don't ask me to tell you, Joy."

"Then I'll ask," Evelyn said "Tell us who did this, Norm. You and I go way back. I understand your motive, but you're better than this."

"It was a weak moment, Evelyn," he said. "I work with folks down at the church who have nothing. I thought if I could make that situation better … I would." He shook his head. "I have no excuse. I'm ready to accept my punishment but I don't want you ladies harmed. So would you just leave, please?"

Joy heard a vehicle drive up and stop outside the garage door. "They're here," Norm whispered. "Get out of here."

"I'm not going anywhere," Joy responded softly but firmly as she moved toward Norm and Evelyn. "I need to see who this is."

Norm shook his head and moved toward the door that led to the warehouse. With one last shake of his head, he flipped the switch to turn off the lights.

"Should we call someone?" Evelyn asked Joy.

"Go back into the warehouse and call 911. I'll stay in here and see who comes in."

"I can't leave you in here," Evelyn protested.

"I'll hide. The police station isn't that far." The garage door screeched as if someone was trying to pull it open. Joy shooed Evelyn away. "It's our chance to catch the thief. Go on and make that call. Tell them it's urgent."

"Hide," Evelyn said to her. "And hide good."

A moment later Evelyn was gone, and Joy was hidden behind a cast-off sofa. The storeroom was in pitch darkness, though a tiny band of light was showing under the garage door behind the statue. More screeching noises, and the door began to open wider. Joy peeked around the end of the sofa.

A man stood in silhouette, the golden rays of the sunset behind him casting his face in shadows. He reached behind the statue, and the room was flooded with light once more.

Apparently there was more than one light switch in this storeroom.

When the man looked up again, Joy edged back into the shadows. Just as she'd suspected.

Richard Bowe.

Chapter Twenty-Two

Joy STEPPED OUT OF HER hiding place. "Hello, Richard," she said calmly. "Did you come to get the statue?"

His expression of shock quickly tempered to a warm smile. "Joy. What are you doing here?"

"I was about to ask you that." She stood in place, aware that Norm and Evelyn were close by and the police were—she hoped—soon to arrive.

"As you said. I came to get the statue. It was stored here at the costume shop in anticipation of the *Night at the Museum* performance tomorrow evening. But unfortunately, the storm has changed those plans."

Richard shifted positions. Behind him gray skies hid the sun.

"Seems like you would want to keep her here until the performance could be rescheduled." She paused. "I'm curious. What does your costume look like?"

His brows gathered, and he looked confused. "My costume? Oh, for the performance?" At her nod, he explained. "I do full top hat and tails for my monologue. It's a throwback to the days when Charleston elite dressed for dinner and gave the best parties."

Joy watched Richard carefully. "With a cape?"

"Yes, of course," he said. "And a top hat and cane. A man was never considered fully dressed without a top hat and cane. I often wonder what it must have been like back then dressed to the nines with all those layers of clothes and no air-conditioning." He shrugged. "I suppose that's why they didn't live as long as we do now."

Richard was rambling, which meant he was nervous.

Emboldened, Joy moved toward the open garage door and leaned forward to look out. Parked just outside was a black pickup.

She committed the license plate to memory and then returned her attention to Richard. "Where are you taking her?" she asked.

Richard smiled. "I thought I'd keep her at my house until she's needed for the performance." His face hardened. "Look, I'm not sure why you're asking me all these questions, but I really need to get on with what I came here for."

He dusted off his clothing then walked over to the statue. "I had this covered," he muttered. "I can't move it like this."

The door to the storeroom opened. "Need some help?"

Richard whirled around toward the sound of Norm's voice. "Hey," he said with a chuckle that held no humor. "I didn't know you were here."

"You weren't supposed to," Norm told him. "Let's see, how was it we moved that thing last time? I believe I took the heavy end. Want me to do that again?"

Richard's eyes widened.

Norm moved closer, coming to stand beside Joy. "You got the jump on me last time, Bowe," he said. "That won't happen today."

"Joy," came Anne's voice. "The lady up front said you and Evelyn were back here. Oh, hi, Richard. She didn't say you were here too."

Richard's eyes darted to Joy and then to Norm. A moment later, he spun around and moved toward the open garage door. There he found Colin Guest blocking his path.

"Colin," Richard said, his voice friendly. "I thought you were busy today."

"I am," he said. "I just came by to check on something."

Richard frowned. "Well, I'll see you at the building site tomorrow. I really need to go."

"He was just leaving," Joy said. "With the Angel of Mercy statue."

Colin looked puzzled. "What are you talking about?"

Richard shook his head. "I don't understand what the big deal is. I never meant for this prop to be stored here. If I leave it someone may think it's available for rent or sale. I don't want anyone to take it."

"Like you did?" Joy said. "And for the record, we know that isn't a prop. That's the real Angel of Mercy statue. The one outside the hospital is an almost perfect fake that Colin sculpted."

"Richard commissioned me to make a copy," Colin said. "He said he wanted it for that performance thing he does. Said it had to be sculpted in secret so everyone would be surprised when they saw it on stage." Realization dawned. "You mean my statue is . . ."

"The one that was put on the base yesterday?" Evelyn supplied from the door. "Yes. Oh, and the police are on their way."

Evelyn's entrance distracted Richard. Norm rushed behind him, and Colin stepped in to subdue the architect long enough for Norm to get handcuffs on him. In the distance, the sound of a police siren wailed.

Richard struggled against the cuffs, but Colin and Norm held him in place. "You'll all be hearing from my lawyer on this. I will not be accused of something I did not do."

Joy looked Richard in the eye. "My guess is you were on your way to sell her."

Richard stared back, his mouth set in a grim line.

Joy continued. "I'm guessing you were hoping to offload the old girl before the storm hit. Am I right?"

Still Richard remained silent. The sound of the siren wailed closer.

"But why?" Anne asked. "What would prompt you to steal the Angel of Mercy statue, Richard? Money, I realize, but why?"

"Because he owes someone money, would be my guess," Joy said. "Flavia was talking to someone on the phone last week when I came into the store. She was upset and said something to the other person about them owing money and not bailing them out this time."

Joy looked at Richard again. "You were asking for money, and your sister turned you down. What I don't understand is why you were asking her for money when you'd already stolen the statue."

"Because I was going to return it, okay?" Richard looked over at Norm, who still held his arm. "I was thinking about what you said, Norm. About how you wanted to use the money for something good but couldn't take it even if it helped others because it was wrong."

Norm shook his head and looked away. "Now he thinks about doing the right thing. Not that I believe you, Richard."

Roots and Wings

"Help me understand why you put Colin's statue into the tunnel," Evelyn said. "Why do that?"

Richard smirked. "That was just a little creativity on my part. It fooled everyone into thinking they had her back, didn't it? Once the fake was found and assumed to be real, I was in the clear and could do what I wanted with the Angel of Mercy."

"But how did you know where the tunnel was?" asked Anne.

"That's easy," Richard said. "The hospital hired me last year to remodel the coffee shop and chapel. Henry gave me tons of blueprints and schematics, and ... I'm a very good architect."

Colin looked stricken. "Mrs. Atkins ... Joy ... you gotta believe me. I didn't know anything about this. I just made a copy of the statue for the performance."

"I believe you," Joy said.

The siren's wail stopped, and car doors opened. "Sounds like your ride is here, Richard," Colin said.

"You can't prove any of this," Richard said, though his voice held little confidence that he believed the words.

Norm's voice broke as he said, "I think the police will believe me."

The storeroom door opened, and two uniformed policemen walked in. Two more officers appeared at the garage door behind the statue. Richard's act was over.

After interviewing everyone, the police took Richard away. Norm confessed his part in the heist. "I did what I did, and I'm a cop. I deserve what's coming to me."

"He subdued a thief," Joy told the officer in charge. "If it hadn't been for Norm, the statue would have been long gone." She looked at

225

Norm. "That's why you were here, wasn't it?" she asked him. "You were trying to save the Angel of Mercy."

"I hoped I could," he said before walking out between two officers.

"Will he be charged?" Anne asked the officer in charge.

"That's up to the DA, ma'am," he said.

Joy led the way back to the parking lot where Evelyn stopped her. "I can't believe Richard took the angel. It's just so hard to wrap my mind around."

"Me too," said Joy. "Although I'd started to have my suspicions, which were only confirmed after we got here and found the statue. Richard's name just kept popping up during our investigation." She counted off on her fingers. "He's Flavia's brother. He knows India and Leticia and has access to Brown Construction Equipment. He had the key to my garage. And he's a Civil War reenactor, which made me think he might have a cape."

"So the guys I saw that night loading the mummy-looking thing into a van were just two guys loading something into a van," said Evelyn.

"They were," Joy said. The wind kicked up, and she looked over at the horizon. "We should be getting home. The storm will be here before daylight tomorrow." She opened her door and looked over the top of the car at Evelyn. "Rob boarded up my windows for me yesterday," she said. "Are y'all ready?"

Evelyn nodded. "James is doing that this morning. I just need to make a quick run to the grocery store, and then I'm set." She groaned. "Although a 'quick' run to the grocery store right before a big storm is pretty much impossible. And who knows if there'll be anything left on the shelves?"

"I need to go to the store too," Anne said.

"Do you mind riding with Anne, Evelyn?" Joy asked. "I need to make a stop on my way home."

Evelyn joined Anne in her car while Joy climbed behind the wheel of hers. She started the engine but didn't make a move to drive away.

After a few minutes, Colin walked out of the costume shop. She climbed out and hurried to meet him.

"Just a couple of things," Joy said when he stopped.

"All right. How can I help you, Mrs. Atkins?"

"The first thing is, I know that you lied to me when you said your aunt took the picture of the rose in my garage. What was that about?"

Colin's face turned red. "Oh, yeah, about that. I'm sorry." He wiped his forehead. "Richard told me to do that. He's the one who sent me the picture. I guess he wanted to throw you off your investigating."

"Well, I appreciate you telling me," Joy said. "The other thing is, your aunt loves you very much." She touched his arm. "I hope you'll find it in your heart to reconcile with her."

He smiled. "Worried about that, are you?"

"I am, actually," Joy told him.

"You don't need to be. She texted me, and I'm on my way to have coffee with her now. I think we'll be okay."

Chapter Twenty-Three

TRUE TO THE WEATHER FORECAST, by late Friday afternoon a storm was still heading toward Charleston. However, there was no hurricane. The winds had calmed, and what would have been Hurricane Joy was downgraded to a mere tropical depression.

"Just a bunch of wind and water," Joy heard more than once from the locals. Still, as the bands of rain pelted the boarded-up windows of her little house, she wondered whether there might be more to it.

At least her garden would be happy with all the water it would get over the next few days. As Joy stood at the front door watching the rain come down in torrents to wash the dust and dirt off Mercy Street, she spied a person tucked under a blue umbrella marked with white clouds walking in her direction. The yellow and white polka-dot slicker suit and red galoshes gave Joy the impression the brave pedestrian was female.

She paused as if looking for a particular address then caught Joy's gaze and smiled. Then she waved.

Angela?

Joy hurried to the door and opened it, grateful for the small sweeping overhang over her head. "Angela! Come in out of the rain, child!"

Angela ducked under the overhang and closed her umbrella then stamped her feet.

"Stay right there, and I'll get a towel," Joy told her.

She hurried to the guest bath upstairs, and smiled at the bathtub that held her portable rose garden for just a few more days. Weather allowing, she would return the roses to India over the weekend.

Grabbing one towel for the floor and two for Angela, she retraced her steps to help manage the task of getting her visitor inside while keeping the storm outside. "Come into the kitchen. I've got coffee brewing," she said when the mission was accomplished.

"Thank you, Mrs. A.," she said. "I hope I'm not intruding."

"Not at all," Joy told her. "I'm glad to see you but wondering why you're out in this weather. Surely you didn't just decide to take a walk."

Angela accepted the mug of coffee with a grateful smile. "Hardly. I parked around the corner on Tradd. I really wanted to speak with you on my way out of town. To thank you for your kindness to me."

"Out of town? I hope your weekend travel takes you to sunnier weather."

Angela took a sip from her mug then said, "It isn't weekend travel. I'm leaving Charleston for now. And that's the other thing I wanted to tell you."

"I don't understand."

She pressed back a damp strand of hair from her face. "I came here to find my family, and in a way, I did. I found their names and the statue that they gave to the city. But as you may know, none of the people I'm related to live in Charleston anymore. So I thought I might go track down a few. Maybe do some more research for the book."

"The book is very exciting," Joy said. "Though I hate to lose you as an assistant. And it won't just be me missing you. So many patients and staff have commented on how much joy you spread at the hospital."

"I'm glad. I'll be back to visit Charleston again, though I can't say when. I heard the original statue will be exchanged for the fake one quietly, so I don't have to attend another ceremony or cut another ribbon. I'm glad about that." She returned her mug to the table and gave Joy a direct look. "I wanted to tell you all along who I was and why I was there. I wish I could have."

"I understand." The rain had slowed now. "I hope you've enjoyed Charleston," Joy said. "You'll be missed. And if you decided to come back for longer than just a visit, I wouldn't be disappointed."

"I've enjoyed myself, but working in the gift shop won't pay the bills, even if I will miss Charleston terribly. Plus Liam is going back to school for the fall semester soon. So I might pay him a visit." Angela looked down at her hands and then back up at Joy. "I better go."

She rose and walked toward the door then donned her damp things. "Oh, before I forget, I came to a dead end in my search for one of my relatives. I was told that Claudia Guest might be able to help. It's my third great-grandmother, I think that's right. The trail has just gone cold for her. Do you know Mrs. Guest well enough to make an introduction? I would like to speak to her, maybe by phone or emails to see what she might know."

"Sure. I have your contact information. I'll ask her if she minds sharing hers with you." Joy paused. "What's the lost relative's name?"

"Octavia," she said. "I think she was from Charleston, and I know she married a Ford, but I never knew for certain anything else about her. Anyway, thanks Mrs. A. See you someday, maybe."

Angela grinned and stepped out into the rain. Joy watched as her new friend's galoshes splashed in the puddles. When Angela turned the corner, Joy retrieved the phone from her pocket and placed a call.

"Claudia," she said, "I have some news for you. Are you sitting down?"

"I'm actually here with Colin and his delightful friend Leticia," she said.

"Then I won't keep you. I just have one question. I think it was mentioned at some point that your family tree has a missing member. Is that correct?"

For a moment Claudia didn't respond. "Yes, actually," she said. "The Butler line is well documented other than a second great-grandmother of mine. It's as if she dropped off the face of the earth."

"Was her name Octavia?"

Claudia gasped. "It was. Why?"

"Because she may have been found." Joy settled onto the chair again. "What would you say if I told you that you could very well be related to Angela Simpson?"

"Joy," she said slowly, "I'm going to need you to explain. Because to be related to Angela would mean ..."

"That you are indeed related to the family responsible for providing the Angel of Mercy for Mercy Hospital. It's just a possibility," Joy said. "Why don't I send you Angela's contact information, and you two can talk?"

"Thank you," Claudia said. "And Joy, I'm so glad you moved here."

"So am I, Claudia," Joy said. "So am I."

Author Letter

Dear Reader,

I hope you've enjoyed walking the halls of Mercy Hospital and the streets of Charleston, South Carolina, as much as I have, figuratively, of course. As I write this, however, I'm planning a trip very soon to walk in the footsteps of Joy, Anne, Evelyn, and Shirley. This time next week, I will be in Charleston! I have a long list of places to see and things to do while I'm there, but I confess that it will be very difficult not to go in search of the Angel of Mercy standing outside Mercy Hospital. You see, the story people in this book have become like friends and the hospital, homes, and businesses like places I've been rather than places I dreamed up.

As with every book, I learned so much. In this story, I had to brush up not only on the city of Charleston and its rich history but also on my knowledge of Noisette roses. Have you heard of them? Noisette roses are beautifully lush roses that originated in Charleston. And guess what? You can't just stick a rose in dirt and hope it will take root. Yes, I learned about how to do that too.

When my research led me to *Southern Living Magazine*, I learned that there really is a local Charleston woman named Stephanie Summerson Hall making beautiful glassware called Estelle's Colored

Glass. This collection is named after her grandmother Estelle, known as Big Mama. Apparently Estelle knew how to set a table at her Sunday dinners, so of course I had to add that touch to my book. You can find out more about this artisan glassware at estellecoloredglass.com.

But most of all, I learned that Joy, Anne, Evelyn, and Shirley are such a fun quartet of accidental sleuths. I cannot wait to see what sort of adventures they will have in future stories in the Sweet Carolina Mysteries series.

I hope you feel the same way.

Enjoy!
—Kathleen Y'Barbo

About the Author

KATHLEEN Y'BARBO IS A BESTSELLING author of more than 100 books. A tenth-generation Texan and certified paralegal, she is a member of numerous professional organizations.

Kathleen and her hero-in-combat-boots husband have their own surprise love story that unfolded on social media a few years back. They now make their home just north of Houston, Texas, and are the parents, grandparents, and in-laws of a blended family of Texans, Okies, and one very adorable trio of Londoners.

The Story Behind the Story

IF YOU KNOW ANYTHING ABOUT roses, you know they come in all shapes, colors, and sizes. In *Roots and Wings*, someone is leaving a rare rose on the base of the Angel of Mercy statue. In order to find out what sort of rose I wanted to use, I had to research roses and narrow it down, not an easy prospect until I discovered the Noisette rose.

Noisette roses are the pale fluffy version of the refined red rose that has come to represent love in bouquets. Unlike that long-stemmed beauty, the Noisette provides a riot of blooms that seem to burst from the stem to full bloom more like a peony than any other sort of rose.

The variety that came to be known as Noisette originated in Charleston, South Carolina, in the early 1800s. Named for Philippe Noisette, a transplanted Frenchman (pun intended), the variety was created by John Champneys when he crossed an Old Blush rose, a pink Chinese rose, and a European musk rose to create a Champneys Pink Cluster rose. From that rose, the Blush Noisette was born. And from the Blush Noisette came the rose from our story.

Two hundred years later the variety of rose known as the Noisette encompasses blooms in shades of pink, pale yellow, white, apricot, and cream. And no, there is no Angel of Mercy Noisette with a red center. That was truly a figment of my imagination.

Noisettes are hardy roses and grow well in Southern climates. If a Noisette is anywhere around, its lovely and heady fragrance will lead you directly to it. These roses begin blooming in spring and carry on through the fall.

To see these beauties in full bloom, check out the Heritage Rose Trail. The Charleston Horticultural Society provides downloadable maps through their website at chashortsoc.org/heritage-rose-society.

Good for What Ails You

Joy Atkins's Mama's Sweet Tea

SET A SAUCEPAN FILLED WITH three cups of cold water onto the stove and turn the burner up to high. Joy's Mama likes the Revereware saucepan she got as a wedding gift, but you can use whatever you've got that's handy. Let that water come to a boil then take it off the stove. Real quick add four Lipton or Luzianne tea bags and let it sit for no more than five minutes. While the water is still hot, remove the tea bags and pour in two cups of sugar, more if you like your tea extra sweet. Stir until all the sugar is mixed in. Pour into your best two-quart tea pitcher—Mama prefers her pale green Depression glass pitcher—and fill to the top with cold water. Put your pitcher into the ice box (yes, it's a refrigerator but that's what Mama always called it) and let it cool until it won't melt all the ice when you pour it. Serve and enjoy!

Joy's Butter Cookies
Ingredients:

1½ cups all-purpose flour, sifted

½ cup cornstarch

½ cup granulated sugar

1 cup softened butter

Instructions:

Preheat oven to 375 degrees F. Grease cookie sheets.

Combine ingredients. Mix well.

Roll 2-inch-sized balls of dough and place 9–12 balls on cookie sheet, evenly spaced. Flatten each with back of fork.

Bake 13 to 15 minutes until light brown. Let cool.

Read on for a sneak peek of another exciting book
in the Sweet Carolina Mysteries series!

Picture-Perfect Mystery
BY RUTH LOGAN HERNE

"YOU MANAGED TO DRAW THE short straw this morning, girlfriend."
Shirley Bashore lifted her brows in sympathy when she spotted
Anne Mabry in the far back corner of the archived records room on
Tuesday morning, a spot not-so-lovingly referred to as the Vault.

Anne wasn't working in the normal records room. That would
be bad enough on a sweltering muggy day like today. The moun-
tainous files gulped the scant AC that permeated these back rooms,
leaving hot, sticky remnants at human level.

Nope.

Today Anne was in the broad, windowless room that rational
people avoided like the plague because it took hot and humid to new
heights. "Aurora has a bee in her bonnet about an article in the
Charleston Buzz that referenced deficient early medical care in our
sweet city and wants me to find facts to refute it."

"Do we care?" asked Shirley. Her tone made it quite clear that
she didn't.

"Not in the least," Anne admitted with a wry smile. "The point of the article was to champion the new Gaylord Cancer Center Infusion Wing opening next week, but you know how historians are," she went on. "Aurora Kingston doesn't just coordinate Mercy Hospital volunteer efforts, she oversees the volunteer fundraising drives for a multitude of events. And when it comes to history and our fair city"—she did a snappy imitation of a cheeky military salute and then sighed—"no one crosses Aurora Kingston. Which means that the new editor of the weekly best not get in the way, having been born and bred in New York City."

"So the editor's new in town? Like me?" asked Shirley. She'd recently come down to Charleston from Atlanta to look after her mother. Regina Bashore had been a registered nurse at Mercy Hospital for decades before her retirement.

Anne went full-bore Southern, knowing the Atlanta-born-and-raised nurse would understand her. "Why, shugah, she's only been here forty-three years. Her daddy came south when manufacturing took a downturn in the North. By our standards that makes her a newcomer. You'll have to live to see ninety-plus to even match her, and you'll still be an import, Shirley. But at least you're Southern," she added cheerfully. "If you have grandchildren born here at some point, they might have a shot at being natives."

Shirley folded her arms across her chest and rolled her eyes. "Anne, I can't even imagine the day when the good Lord gives me time to fuss about such things. I'm on my way down the hall to get iced coffee, and I knew you were trapped. Can I get you a nice tall latte or sweet tea?"

That was the first thing Anne had learned about Shirley when she came on board in April. She went out of her way to be kind, and that endeared the African American woman to the rest of the crew working Mercy Hospital's main floor between the emergency room, the beautifully renovated main lobby, and the historic arm of Mercy Hospital known as the Angel Wing. When the historic hospital had suffered a devastating mid-nineteenth-century fire, the only wing that survived was the one guarded by the locally well-known angel statue. The wing had been modernized and refurbished, but the history and the statue remained intact. The summer started on a rocky note, with the angel statue's disappearance, but the statue was back in its rightful place, and that was a good thing. Mercy Hospital hadn't felt right or whole without it.

"A latte," she told Shirley. "As big as they've got, short on ice, heavy on espresso. I've got to get this stuff found, and an ice-cold coffee would hit the spot. On the plus side, Addie is at camp until a week from Sunday, so I can tackle this and not feel the need to rush home." Anne loved her volunteer position at the historic Charleston hospital but also loved her newest responsibility. She and her husband, Ralph, were caring for their beautiful granddaughter while their daughter Lili was deployed. The girl was an absolute treat, and beloved, but her being at riding camp gave Anne a broader window of time to get things done, and that was nice too.

"She is the sweetest child." Shirley's voice softened.

"She is, isn't she?" Anne mellowed her voice too, because there was something special and youthful about taking on a busy seven-year-old with thoughts and ideas of her own. "She invigorates us.

Me, especially, because you know that Ralph's time here at the hospital has grown since he retired from his pastoral duties at St. Michael's."

"Horning in on his pretty wife's gig, that's what I say," Shirley teased.

"I can't disagree," Anne agreed. "I love that man, but sometimes a pastor's wife needs a distraction and that's what Mercy Hospital has been for me. Volunteering here was my way of giving back and kept me a little bit sideways of the congregation. It all worked better with that window of space. But time marches on and my hideaway has been infiltrated by my industrious and kind-hearted husband." Anne pulled a cabinet door open and sneezed three times as the dust tickled her nose. Eyes running, she groaned and snatched a handful of tissues from an equally dusty box nearby. "One of these days I'm going to hide out in this room and just dust, dust, dust. If I do that, Evelyn will happily tackle the necessary reorganization."

"And I'm steering clear of the mess," noted Shirley with a slanted look toward the nearby tabletop, "but I'll be right back with your coffee, Sweetness."

Anne blotted her nose and waved her thanks.

The nickname made her smile. Shirley had dubbed her that during her first weeks on the job, and the name had struck a chord between them. Finding a fast friend wasn't an easy task, and it didn't grow easier with age, which made her quick friendship with Shirley a true blessing. She stooped low and reached into the cabinet marked HISTORICAL RECORDS AND REPORTS. A thin layer of dust coated the inside of the cabinet too.

She dampened a paper towel with a spray bottle and swept it across the shelf before withdrawing a thick bundle of folders and news clippings. She set them on the table. She retrieved several more stacks from the lower shelves then paused when her hand bumped something flat and hard.

She set the folders down then crouched real low. She got so low that she blessed her daily workout routine because regular exercise was the only thing that made it possible to half crawl into the stupid cabinet to retrieve this last object.

Grasping the front corner, she nudged the object forward.

A box.

And not a regular box, not a cardboard box filled with musty papers, the unfortunate norm in many of these metal storage cabinets.

It was a wooden box, plain and old. Really old. Anne had a measure of respect for old things, but she was more a farm chic kind of decorator, so their cozy bungalow not far from Addie's school was done in warm ivories with splashes of color. But this—

She set the box on the table then perched on one of the three stools that had been thick with dust when she walked in. She'd wiped them down first thing, and she'd just opened the box when Shirley came in with their drinks. Evelyn Perry came in behind her and lifted her brows in surprise when she spotted the box. "What's that? And what's it doing in the Vault?"

Evelyn Perry had been Anne's friend for years, and it was Evelyn who talked Anne into doing hospital volunteer work over three decades before. Evelyn was in charge of the current records room, situated between these archives and the busy ER admissions desk and waiting area. "No clue," Anne told her. She nudged the metal cabinet door shut with her foot so that no one would bump their leg against it. "It was buried in the farthest corner of this wretchedly overstuffed cabinet. Tucked so far back that if I hadn't practically crawled into the cabinet, I wouldn't have seen it." With gloved hands, she slowly raised the lid.

Anne thought the box would smell musty.

It didn't.

And with the top raised, several old, folded-up papers and a host of photographs came into view. All black-and-white, except three, toward the bottom. Those were in full color and not badly faded.

"Anne, I can't imagine what this is all about," said Evelyn as she and Shirley watched. "But then," she continued, "I've made it a point to stay as far away from those cabinets as I can. Something about deep dark recesses repels my good nature. Although I have pledged to do something about this room. It's out of control." Evelyn liked organization, and if it didn't exist, she'd make sure it happened. The vintage records room overhaul had made her summer short list.

"This is very interesting," said Shirley, peeking over Anne's shoulder. "Some of those pictures look to be nearly a century old, but I don't see anything to do with the hospital, then or now. Do you?" she queried the other ladies.

Evelyn slipped one of the ever-present pencils from her updo and lifted several photos with the eraser end. "Not a thing. They seem to be shots done at school, perhaps. This one, with these young ladies sitting at tables? Definitely a school setting, wouldn't you say? Even these others seem to be school related. The children playing.

The old brick of that building." She pointed to a corner of the building at one side.

Shirley took a paper from the box, unfolded it, and drew a sharp breath.

"What is it, Shirl?" Anne reached out a hand.

"Looks like a treasure map," said Shirley as she handed it over. "Written on the back of an old prescription paper, so that makes it even more authentic. *X* marks the spot."

"Treasure map?" Anne accepted the paper, studied it, and then handed it to Evelyn as she and Shirley unfolded the other two sheets of matching paper.

"A poem." Anne flipped the prescription paper over, revealing the first part of a verse. "'The kiss of the sun for pardon, The song of the birds for mirth—'"

"'One is nearer God's heart in a garden,'" continued Shirley from her paper. "'Than anywhere else on Earth.'"

"Oh, that's lovely," said Evelyn softly. "Despite my lack of finesse in the garden, that touches my heart. And my soul."

"It's odd to have this written on two sheets instead of one, though," mused Anne. "A game, maybe? Because all three are on the same kind of paper. Pharmaceutical paper, and nothing too recent either."

"For kids to find a treasure," declared Evelyn. She was childless, but she and her history-loving husband were beloved by a slew of other people's children. A fair share of them called Evelyn "Grandma Evie," and she loved the title. "Absolutely innovative, wouldn't you agree?"

"But who in their right mind would hide scribblings of a kids' game in a box, in the back of the lowest shelf of a cabinet that no one ever ventured into?" Shirley didn't sound convinced. "That makes no sense."

"With pictures," noted Evelyn. "The only pictures I'd expect to find in here would be hospital functions, and if my sinuses didn't go into full meltdown over dust, I'd have this room in shipshape order already. But"—her eyes began to water right then—"not without a good cleaning and an allergy pill. What's that you've got, Anne?" she asked as Anne held a picture aloft. She reached for a tissue but, given the dust on the tissue box, must have changed her mind. She sniffled.

"Romance," breathed Anne, holding the picture up for Shirley and Evelyn to see. "Look at these two. The longing in their eyes. That expression of—" She paused then stood up and moved toward the light. When she got beneath it, she extended the picture out to brighten the image. "Byron Wellington."

"Who?" Shirley asked as Evelyn moved toward Anne.

Evelyn put her reading glasses into place and looked as surprised as Anne felt. "He sure looks like Byron, but Byron is our age or a bit younger," she reminded Anne. "The man in this picture was in his late twenties or early thirties, don't you think? Byron's father, maybe? Because the resemblance is striking, I see it, plain as day."

"Grandfather, more likely," said Shirley as she glanced at her watch and moved toward the door connecting the records area to the archives. "He'd be at least a hundred and twenty by now, judging from the date on the back and there aren't many men out there having babies in their sixties. Especially not back then," she added. "Duty calls. I'm off to work, my friends. See you later."

"Thanks for the latte, Shirley." Anne said. "I'm buying next time."

"And I'll let you." Shirley hurried off with a wave, and Evelyn turned back toward the pictures. "This is weird, Anne."

It was.

Not just finding a box in a recessed corner but finding a box with personal artifacts that had nothing to do with the hospital. "You see the resemblance, don't you?"

"Vividly," agreed Evelyn. "But Byron left under such awful circumstances that I can't imagine why this would be here. What it means. Or why—"

Anne lifted the last folded paper in the box, tucked beneath the photographs. These sheets were full-size and folded in thirds like an official business letter. There were three pages stapled together. As she unfolded the front-facing paper, four meaningful words jumped out at her, done in fancy type, scrolled across the top quarter of the paper. And when she read those words, she looked from the document to Evelyn and whistled softly. "Good night, nurse! It's someone's will, Evie." She pointed to the date. "1991. What on earth is it doing here?" she wondered.

Evelyn leaned over and read the will out loud in a soft voice. "'I, Richard Byron Wellington, do hereby bequeath the sum of three thousand dollars to each of these grandchildren: Dale Wellington, Patience Wellington Connors, Susannah Montgomery, Abel Jackson, and Adrianna Jackson Summers. The remainder of my estate and all of my physical properties and real estate are hereby bequeathed to my oldest grandson, Dr. Byron Michael Wellington, who always understood the value of education and stopped at nothing to achieve it. If bequests are not freely accepted through the law firm of Morris,

Morris & Whitaker within thirty years, all rights will revert to the Greater Charleston Preservation Society to do with as they deem fit. Signed by me, this seventh day of August, in the year of Our Lord 1991.'"

It was signed, *Richard Byron Wellington, Esquire*

Two witness names were scrawled beneath Richard Wellington's signature, and the paper bore the official seal of having been accepted as a legal document—but was it still legal and binding?

Anne had no idea. "Evelyn, what do you think? Do you think Dr. Wellington ever got this? Or even knew about it? It was written about the same time he disappeared. Unless…" Anne's breath caught in her throat. "Unless someone knew about this thirty-year clause and Byron didn't just walk away." A thought that had never once crossed her mind crossed it now. "Maybe someone made him disappear."